Praise for

STATIONS
PAINTINGS & POEMS OF SPIRITUAL JOURNEY

    In our time, feminists are taking up the cross in new liberating ways. In this work of art Mary and Norman have juxtaposed the Stations of the Cross with an incredible array of contemporary, traditional and biblical persons and events: Scots and Presbyterians alongside the women in Genesis; Nicaragua and the deaths of dogs; Violations of women and children and the destruction of creation. The layered traditions of the Via Dolorosa itself — Muslim, Crusade, European are juxtaposed with the stories and allusions of the re-visionist poems. Grace is intertwined with sin; hope, faith and love with the Fall. Like Jesus' journey, our journey must catch up and recapitulate the human story, breaking down time and cultural walls, drawing the reader into the costly grace of Christ. This is an artistic event of solidarity with those who suffered, suffer and will suffer.

Stuart D. McLean
Associate Professor of Christian Ethics, Phillips Graduate Seminary

    The images and poetry of these pages invite us into the horrors of human suffering, and the inhumanity of inflicted crosses. In an age when we are beginning to understand more clearly the oppressive impact of North American theologies of sacrifice, these stations of the cross do not romanticize crucifixions, but compel us to resist them.With powerful language, and subtle image, we are drawn into the full weight of human pain, and are urgedto take our stand beside those who understand that crosses are rooted not in self-sacrifice, but profound, transforming solidarity. No humanbeing should have to endure a cross, and no human heing should have to endure the evil that produces it. The poet and painter here use the traditional stations of the cross as a spiritual tool that will empower us to endure them no longer.

Christine Marie Smith
Assoc. Prof, of Preaching and Worship United Theological Seminary of the Twin Cities

    Mary McAnally is a pilgrim and a poet. How fortunate we are to accompany her on the Via Dolorosa.   Fortunate also to have these artful illuminations of the route by painter Norman Dolph. They take us to places where they have been, and many of them appear familiar to us as well. We follow Christ and stop with him at fourteen stations. We are redeemed by the poetry of his cross. And religious poetry is redeemed along the way.

Bro. Benet Tvedten, O.S.B.
Blue Cloud Abbey,Marvin, S.Dakota

The Authors

Rev. Mary McAnally
Raised in Tulsa, studied at the University of Tulsa (B.A. Hon.), Princeton Theological Seminary, Columbia University / Teachers College Graduate School (M.A. and residency for Ph.D.), and Phillips Graduate Seminary(M.Div. magna cum laude). A poet published widely in literary journals and anthologies, she has five chapbooks of her own poetry, and has edited five anthologies, including a collection of poems by her prisoner students, and one on family violence that is used in group therapy in shelters across the nation. Received National Endowment for the Arts Creative Writing Literary Fellowship in 1981 - 82 for two of her manuscripts now in chapbooks. Activist for peace and justice issues, feminist theologian, and mother of two, Mary was pastor of Westminster Presbyterian Church in Tulsa, Oklahoma till Easter 1994, was for 20 years part time Chaplain at Hillcrest Hospital, Volunteer Services Coordinator and Chaplain at Tulsa Community Corrections Center (a local, co-ed prison), and part time Clinical Supervisor at First Wings of Freedom, a residential drug and alcohol treatment center for women with children. Since 1994 she has worked part-time as counselor and clergy care for Reproductive Services Clinic in Tulsa, Oklahoma's only nonprofit abortion clinic. She currently serves as Board President of the Oklahoma Religious Coalition for Reproductive Choice, State Coordinator of Pastors for Peace, and 35-year Precinct Officer of the Democratic Party. She has pastored one Presbyterian and two Unitarian congregations. Widow of poet Etheridge Knight, she is mother of Mary Tandiwe McAnally, Etheridge Bambata McAnally, and grandmother of Kevin Montez McAnally, Miles Davis McAnally, Romello McAnally and Belzora Himiko McAnally.

Norman Dolph
Born in Tulsa, was graduated from Yale University, lives in New York City. Raised as a Disciple of Christ, he has served as a Presbyterian Elder. In addition to painting, he is an award winning lyricist and software developer. His work is in New York, London, Boston and Los Angeles collections. The idea for *Stations* was inspired by Barnett Newman's abstract, black and white *Stations of the Cross*, as shown in the National Gallery in Washington. The idea was transferred to canvas after Norman made a pilgrimage to Jerusalem in 1991 to photograph the sites. The paintings were completed, using the photographs as inspiration, in his New York studio in 1992. They are executed in a polymer resin ink directly onto raw canvas, and are 54" by 40" in size. The paintings were selected as part of the International Biannual Exhibit of Sacred Art in Teramo, Italy in June and July, 1994. They may be seen in greater detail at stationsofthecross.net.

NORMAN DOLPH and MARY McANALLY were classmates at Will Rogers High School in Tulsa, Oklahoma, and have remained friends and colleagues throughout the years.

STATIONS
Paintings & Poems of Spiritual Journey

Rev. Mary McAnally
Poet

Norman Dolph
Painter

Inspired by
The Stations of the Cross

GoodReadBooks™, Inc.
"Reading Is Time Well Spent"

STATIONS - Paintings & Poems of Spiritual Journey

Copyright © 2013 by GoodReadBooks™, Inc. All rights reserved. Printed in the United States of America. No part of this book may be used or reproduced in any manner whatsoever without written permission, except in the case of brief quotations embodied in critical articles and reviews.
For information, contact: Service@GoodReadBooks.com

At the publisher's discretion, GRB's books may be purchased at a discount for educational, business, or sales promotional use. For information please contact Service@GoodReadBooks.com

First Printing of 20th Anniversary "Resurrection" Edition
Published New York City, NY, USA

Catalog Information:

Author: McAnally, Rev. M.E.
Painter/Illustrator: Dolph, N.E.
Poetry - Art - Christian Theology - Jerusalem - Stations of the Cross
Title: STATIONS Paintings & Poems of Spiritual Journey

ISBN: 978-0-9777512-0-4 (Trade Paperback Edition)
ISBN: 978-0-0777512-1-1 (Amazon Kindle Edition)

ASIN: B00I764SSO
LCCN: 2013951619

6 5 4 3 2 1

Contents

Foreword	v
Acknowledgments	vii
Credits and Other Publications	vii
Jerusalem in the Time of Jesus	viii
Introduction	ix
The Pathway	xx

Station One: The Verdict ... 1
   "Bare"ing the Sins of the Fathers ... 5
   Ecce Homo ... 7

Station Two: Jesus Takes Up The Cross ... 8
   Taking Up The Cross ... 11
   Woman Rising ... 12
   Amartia ... 13

Station Three: Jesus Falls for the First Time ... 14
   FIRST FALL ... 17
   SYZYGY ... 17
   Our Mother's Body Is The Earth ... 18

Station Four: Jesus Encounters His Mother Mary ... 20
   Annunciation ... 23
   Rebekah's Poem ... 23

Station Five: Simon of Cyrene Helps Carry The Cross ... 24
   Help ... 27

Station Six: The Woman Wipes His Bloody Brow ... 28
   The Saint of the True Image ... 31
   Imago Dei ... 31

Station Seven: Jesus Falls A Second Time ... 32
   THE FALL ... 34

Station Eight: Jesus Comforts the Women ... 36
   Dinah ... 39
   Jesus Addresses Miriam ... 40
   Lot's Wife ... 41
   Lot's Daughters ... 41
   Taste Its Bleeding ... 42
   Couvade For Jephthah's Daughter ... 43

Station Nine: Jesus Falls A Third Time 44
    When The Body Fails Us 47
    Code Blue 47

Station Ten: The Dividing Of The Garments 48
    The Seamless Robe 51

Station Eleven: The Crucifixion 52
    The Reckoning 55
    The Dog Who Dreamed Of Dying 56
    Sophia Mandala 57

Station Twelve: Jesus Dies 58
    The Place of a Skull 61
    Hunger Strikes 62
    Bathsheba's Confession 63

Station Thirteen: Jesus' Body Is Taken Down From The Cross 64
    Doomsday 67
    Life After Death? 68

Station Fourteen: Jesus' Body Is Laid In The Tomb 69
    Stations 76
    Honest To God . . . There Are Days 82

Afterword 84

Bibliography 87

Foreword

Sometimes Protestants forget that for the first fourteen centuries or so of Christendom there was just one church, and the history of that one church is also our history. Even though it separated later into Roman Catholic, Eastern (Greek and Russian) Orthodox, and Protestant, at one time we were united.

Needless to say, it is the prayer of many Christians of all branches of Christendom that we will one day again be united, at least in Spirit if not in practice and polity.

One of the elements of earlier Christian worship was an emphasis on the Stations of the Cross not only as the path Jesus took to Golgotha, but as a metaphor for spiritual journey for those who follow him (see the Afterword for more detail on this). Reformed Christians may find in this metaphor a valuable experience for their own faith or spiritual development. Norman and I have certainly done so, as have many others before us.

St. Bonaventure teaches that there are

...three parallel paths leading to perfection: the purgative way, which eliminates sin; the illuminative way, which proposes the virtues of Christ as the antidote for sin and the vices of fallen man (sic); and the unitive way, which through union with Christ conquers evil and makes perfect ....Each station will therefore, after a brief consideration of the subject, apply the lesson of the Station to the interior life according to the purgative, the illuminative, and the unitive way."

(Leo Beuthey, *The Way of the Cross*. Illinois: Franciscan Herald Press, 1956, Foreword, pp. iv-v.)

John Calvin conjoins that suggestion with his own opening to the first chapter of his *Institutes* by saying that "nearly all the wisdom we possess, that is to say, true and sound wisdom, consists of two parts: the knowledge of God and of ourselves". It is the search for that knowledge, or "The Holy Grail", that constitutes spiritual journey or faith development. (The name of that wisdom, by the way, is Sophia, the Greek term used for it over 250 times in the Bible.)

While Norman was struggling up the Via Dolorosa in Jerusalem, I was struggling with new, poetic interpretations of some biblical events, characters, and stories. My own journey has been a search for linguistic images to describe my relationship with God and the world. So some of these poems were written while Norman was doing his painting. Others came later after he shared his paintings and story with me.

A key experience in Norman's spiritual life was his own trip to Israel when he retraced the Via Dolorosa with the eye of the artist/painter. During that time also, he experienced a near miracle relating to his own health. He brought the Via Dolorosa experience home to roost in my heart also, though I have never been there physically. As a result, we decided to collaborate on this volume.

Norman says you need to be in three places at one time: at the event 2,000 years ago, at the present site on the Via Dolorosa in Jerusalem, and at the spot where you, the reader, are now standing in your own life journey.

First, you are asked to read the scriptural references and invoke in your mind's eye the events that took place long ago. Try to exorcise from your imaginings the Hollywood renditions you might have seen of those events.

Then examine the artist's painting of the actual site today with all its implications. (For example, Station I: the courtyard where Jesus was tried, reviled, and beaten is now the playground of a Muslim boy's school. What ideas and images does that fact conjure in your imagination? What connections or disconnections can you see, or what ironies or scandals does it invoke? What does it say about beginnings? About Abraham's first-born, Ishmael, and Ishmael's brother Isaac, and the Arab-Israel conflict?)

Finally, allow the poems to carry your imagination into other realms of discovery. Let the magic of the word speak to or for you.

Both paintings and poems express the experiences and searchings of the artist but might also serve as a kind of road map to aid your own search. As the paintings address you visually, the poems address you viscerally. Together they seek a new language of vision and revelation (heuresis).

Spiritual journey has certain requirements. Jesus required of his disciples only a walking stick. This journey requires an open heart and mind, a longing to learn and grow, to make a better world. Such journeys are often postponed, but can never be totally ignored or bypassed. They take courage, commitment, strength and determination. Sometimes you have to backtrack and start over. Sometimes you get lost. You may often feel very alone. But the Psalmist reminds us that even when we walk through the valley of the shadow of death, we need fear nothing, God is with us. (Psalm 23)

This book provides at least 14 opportunities for you to stop and think. Hopefully at the end of the book you will feel some small light has been cast on your own spiritual path. At 12 of the 14 steps, references have been included from the 12-step program of Alcoholics Anonymous (AA) as additional opportunities for reflection.

--Mary McAnally

All scriptural references are from the New Revised Standard Version of the Bible.

Acknowledgments

Special thanks to the following for their moral support, encouragement, and other invaluable assistance in making this manuscript possible: Meridel LeSueur, whose critiques and advice contributed greatly to its integrity; Will Inman, whose poems so inspired me that lines from them have demanded reiteration in my poems; Brother Benet, whose quiet prayers and gentle proddings have inspired this work and my own decision to become an Oblate of St. Benedict; Bill Turley, whose excellent and efficient research in the Blue Cloud Abbey library contributed immensely to the prose sections (especially the Afterword); the nuns at the Forest of Peace who gave me sanctuary for my writing; my mother, Mary Frances Ruble, who financed our 1990 trip to El Salvador and Nicaragua and has been a lifelong guide and friend; Carole Brown, whose gift of typesetting and design helped me believe the book would finally come to print; the friends who wrote the supportive blurbs; and the countless other women before me, unnamed, unsung women, and those who follow, form Bible times to the New Age, God bless you all. I love you.

The reader is referred to *The Twelve Steps — A Spiritual Journey: A Working Guide for Adult Children From Addictive and Other Dysfunctional Families - Based on Biblical Teachings* (San Diego, CA: Recovery Publications, 1980).

Credits and Other Publications

Rev. Mary McAnally

The following chapbooks of poetry have been published:

We Will Make a River (Cambridge, MS: West End Press, 1978)
Poems From the Animal Heart (Edmond, OK: Full Count Press, 1981)
The Absence of the Father and the Dance of the Zygotes (Minneapolis, MN: Shadow Press, 1982)
Coming of Age in Oklahoma (Norman, OK: Point Riders Press, 1988)
Fat Poems (Tulsa, OK: Cardinal Press, 1990)
Thin Places, Poems from a Benedictine Pilgrimage to Ireland (The Open Door Press, 2002)
Cosmic Rainbow, New and Selected Poems (Partisan Press, 2006)
The 2nd and 3rd chapbooks above were funded by the National Endowment for the Arts.

Edited the following anthologies:

New Black Writing (Tulsa, OK: Nimrod, 1978)
Warning Hitchhikers May Be Escaping Convicts (La Jolla, CA: Moonlight Publications, 1981) anthology of prison poetry
Family Violence: Poems on the Pathology (La Jolla, CA: Moonlight Publications, 1982) - anthology of poems about family violence
We Sing Our Struggle (Tulsa, OK: Cardinal Press, 1982)- anthology paying tribute to radical writer, Meridel LeSueur

Received the following literary awards:

Beaudoin Gem Stone Prize for Poetry, 1978
Carl Sandburg Poetry Prize (Dept. of the Interior), 1979
National Endowment for the Arts Creative Writing Fellowship, 1981-82

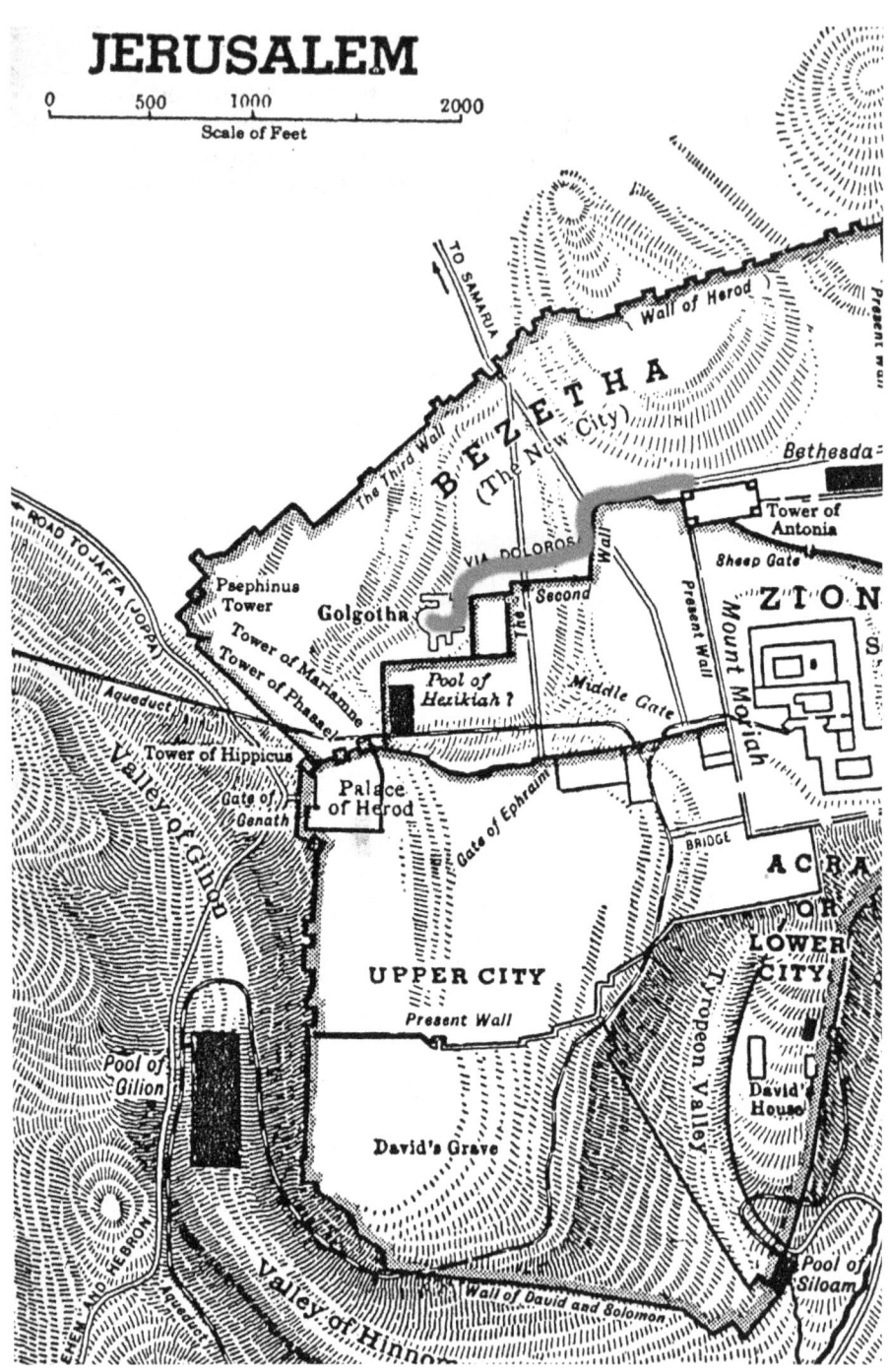

JERUSALEM IN THE TIME OF JESUS

Introduction

It is crucial to say something here about religious language. One of the most radically religious books written in our century was Alice Walker's Pulitzer Prize-winning novel *The Color Purple*. It was a series of letters to God written by a young tum-of-the-century illiterate black girl in her own stumbling, gritty, raw speech. Her letters to God were like prayers about her father molesting her and kidnapping her baby, and her husband abusing her. Yet several communities tried to get it banned from the public schools as pornographic.

How else can someone write about the obscenities of child abuse and incest, babynapping, and wife beating, except in raw, obscene language? How do we talk or write about God and ourselves? Poetry about lovely maidens dancing in the moonlight just doesn't do it. On the first page of Chapter I, "Introduction: To Speak Rightly About God," in Elizabeth Johnson's monumental work *She Who Is· The Mystery of God* in Feminist Theological Discourse (New York: Crossroad, 1993) she asks the question:

> "What is the right way to speak about God? This is the question of unsurpassed importance, for speech about the mystery that surrounds human lives and the universe itself is a key activity of a community of faith." (pp. 3-4)

She carefully and painstakingly articulates her answer. In a scholarly and visionary exploration she provides some historical background to the dilemma of God-talk, some basic linguistic options, and some new insights into the Wisdom (Sophia) manifestation of God.

Feminist theologian after feminist theologian in the last century has tried to explain the very nature of God-talk (see particularly Rita Nakashima Brock, Mary Collins, Mary Daley, Joan Chamberlain Engelsman, Francis Schussler Fiorenza, Carol Gilligan, Elizabeth Dodson Gray, Sallie McFague, Virginia Ramey Mollenkott, Mercy Amba Oduyoye, Rosemary Radford Ruether, Letty Russell, Starhawk, Phyllis Trible, and Miriam Therese Winter, to name just a few). Many of these women writers, and some contemporary male theologians also, suggest that quite possibly it is poets who have a unique prophetic gift for God talk, namely, the gift of metaphorical thought and language.

Johnson devotes ten pages of her concluding chapter of *She Who Is* to "Female Metaphors" for God (pp. 254-264). Understanding metaphor is the gift that allows the poetic imagination to make the leap from one reality to another without falling into the chasm between. It takes a particular mind-set to be able to live in the creative tension of the metaphor.

God-talk, or religious language, is clearly at the crux of this century's issues and crises, and an understanding of metaphor is at the crux of religious language. One poet friend of mine, Bill Turley, said it another way. He said the main problem facing poets in the 21st century is the problem of the impersonal pronoun. Little did he know that his comment made in the 70s would define a major theological conundrum in the 80s and 90s as theological seminaries and denominational publications and even Bible translations(!) have attempted to use more inclusive language due to the insistence of feminists.

Take the central metaphor of Christianity, for example: 'Jesus is God. Jesus is not God." The great mystery embodied in these statements, which must necessarily appear together, is the basis of Christian faith and life. Both statements are true. Yet each statement is also false. Early creeds attempted in their limited ways to describe this indescribable reality (for example, the Nicene Creed). It takes a creative and also adventuresome Christian to be able to live with such conflicting truths. It takes someone who understands the nature of language itself as symbolic and metaphorical, and not simply literalistic. It takes some one who can live with mystery, allowing some things, like God, to exist beyond our abilities to describe or prescribe.

Such is the nature of language. Methuselah lived 900 years. "It ain't necessarily so," the song insists from Porgy and Bess. And so all the language about God over the centuries that has come to be accepted as absolute, "literal" truth, as final formulation, as perfect explanation, "ain't necessarily so." God simply cannot be bagged up and bundled in mere human terms, formulas or doctrines. As history changes, and humans change, so our concept of God changes, enlarges, transmutes, emerges, convolutes, alters. Some call God Yahweh, Jehovah, Sophia, El Shaddai, Shekinah, Elohim. Others call God Rock, Fortress, Pillar, Wind and Fire. Still others call God Shepherd, Light of the World, Bread, Prince of Peace, Friend, Lover of my Soul. Whatever name means something to you, call it.

If referring to God as "Father" only reminds you of that large man taking off his belt and coming toward you on the bed, or the one who molested you or beat your mother or abandoned the family, then call God "Mother" if referring to God as "Mother" helps you worship her better. And if you shudder to hear God referred to as "her", why not try to identify with those who shudder when they hear God referred to only as "him"?

As Elizabeth Johnson reminds us in *She Who Is*, even Aquinas defended the use of extra-biblical language about God on grounds of historical necessity: "The urgency of confuting heretics made it necessary to find new words to ex press the ancient faith about God ... Nor is such a kind of novelty to be shunned; since it is by no means profane, for it does not lead us astray from the sense of scripture." (p. 6) The most adamantly promoted formula for God-- the Trinity-- is not even found as such in scripture, but came into existence around the 4th century. Yet ironically it is the biblical literalists who most often denounce any divergence from a Trinitarian concept as heresy.

Johnson goes on to insist that:

It is not necessary to restrict speech about God to the exact names that Scripture uses, nor to terms coined by the later tradition. So long as the words signify something that does characterize the living God mediated through Scripture, tradition, and present faith experience, for example, divine liberating action or self-involving love for the world, then new language can be used with confidence. (p. 7)

She also reminds us of "Augustine's insight that if we have understood, then what we have understood is not God; Anselm's argument that God is that than which nothing greater can be conceived" and "Aquinas's working rule that we can know that God is and what God is not, but not what God is". (p. 7)

I often invite my poet friends to my home with the comment, "Let's get together and tell some lies." They always chuckle. They know what I mean. Doing poetry is both telling lies and telling great truths in new ways. Poetry is metaphor. This is why the Bible itself should be read as poetry. Indeed, much of it was clearly written by poets: The Song of Solomon, Daniel, Isaiah, Psalms, Proverbs, The Gospel According to John, the Book of Revelation. Perhaps all of it. Or at least by writers who understood the symbolic nature of language.

The Bible holds both the greatest truths and the subtlest deceptions. We are given the gift of discernment, the most important of the scripture's gifts: to know which is which. Try humans. Now let the Spirit of discernment or Wisdom (Sophia!) help you understand why both these statements are true, both false.

It should be no surprise that poets have always attempted the dangerous task of renaming God. Four decades ago, Pulitzer Prize-winning Chilean poet, Nicanor Parra, wrote a poem called "Changes of Name" in which he said,

I am going to change the names of some things. My position is this: The poet is not true to his word if he doesn't change the names of things....

God too must have his name changed. Let each person call him what he will. That is a personal problem

(Poems and Antipoems, Edited by William Miller, New York: New Directions, 1958, p. 65)

(Please note the masculine impersonal pronouns!)

If you wish to know God better, it would help to understand metaphor. Sallie McFague affirms this in *Metaphorical Theology: Models of God in Religious Language* (Philadelphia: Fortress Press, 1982). She says that

> ...poetry and religion, the two fields which have always known they must think via metaphor (and as a consequence have been denied by many as dealing in knowledge-- truth and meaning), now find that their way of metaphor and indirection is widely accepted as necessary in all creative, constructive thought. (p. 25)

There are simply some truths that are too deep for words, such as the kiss of a lover, the glory of a magnificent sunset, the undulating wedge-shaped migratory flight of a group of snow geese-- such as God. The poetry language of the Psalms mentions "deep speaking to deep" (42:7). It is for such deep things that metaphor is required. Only metaphor has within it both truth and untruth. This is why it is necessary to use metaphor to describe God: because no description of God could ever be "the truth, the whole truth and nothing but the truth." To experience, understand, and communicate with and about God better, we must all be in the business of creating new metaphors, new religious language and symbols.

It should be obvious to all that not only should metaphor be used in God language, it is unsubstitutable. Literalistic language can NEVER be used to describe God, or Jesus Christ, or the Spirit, or faith, or any of the other "deep" truths of spiritual reality. To say "God is love" is to utter one of the most provocative and perfect metaphors. But it must be accompanied by other metaphors, because "God is love" says very little about God as Judge or Destroyer.

One of the principal contemporary theorists on metaphor as unsubstitutable language is I. A. Richards, who writes that "when we use a metaphor we have two thoughts of different things active together and supported by a single word, or phrase, whose meaning is a resultant of their interaction." I. A. Richards, *The Philosophy of Rhetoric.* New York: Macmillan Co. 1962, pp. 42-43.)

Walter Brueggemann suggests that the poet/prophet (contemporary comedians might call them "metaphormeisters") is the best preacher of the good news. In *Finally Comes the Poet: Daring Speech for Proclamation* (Minneapolis, MN: Fortress Press, 1989.) Brueggemann quotes Hans Urs von Balthasar, Roman Catholic scholar: "God needs prophets in order to make himself (sic.) known, and all prophets are necessarily artistic. What a prophet has to say can never be said in prose." (p. 4) Brueggemann goes even further to say that "the act of sacrament requires the speech of poetry to keep hidden what must not be profaned by description." (p. 27) He says that "only a poet can speak both dimensions of our dangerous way with God ..." (p. 39)

"This is my body, broken for you." Only such a metaphor could be uttered during Holy Communion, because only a metaphor contains within it the possibility that the wafer is his body and is not his body. Deny the metaphor — deny BOTH realities — and what you have left is either a cannibalistic ritual on the one hand, or an empty, meaningless one on the other. Donald Capps takes this idea even further in *The Poet's Gift: Toward the Renewal of Pastoral Care* (Louisville: Westminster/John Knox Press. 1993). He uses the parable, the primary method Jesus used for teaching and preaching, which is pure narrative metaphor (or metaphorical narrative), to describe how the therapist can use narrative (life story) in healing. Jesus purposefully preached and taught in parables because of their unique ability to be translated, interpreted or applied in diverse ways, thus rendering them more universally accessible.

In our time, feminist poets, artists, and theologians are the prophets and priestesses who are in the forefront of the transformation of the church and the world as they are led by God's Spirit of Wisdom (Sophia) to be and do so. The most important way this is taking place is by the transformation of our language and of our understanding of language. However, they are being met with great resistance, both outside and within the church. A powerful example of this resistance can be found in some reactions to a conference held in Minnesota in November 1993. The openly feminist conference was part of the World Council of Churches' Decade of Churches in Solidarity With Women, and was an ecumenical, international gathering around the theme "Re-Imagining". Over 2,200 women and 83 men from more than 20 religious traditions gathered to "re-imagine" God. For four days they prayed, studied, sang, danced, discussed and debated, heard speeches and sermons, and demonstrated to the world, by their love for God and for one another, the reality of unity in diversity in Christendom. Most shared an experience of God's Spirit at the conference that led them to make deeper commitments to work for peace and justice in the world and in the church.

Reactive, fundamentalist elements in at least four "mainline" denominations have sought the ouster of conference planners, leaders, and participants from positions of leadership in the church, and even from pulpits or congregations. Some have been "fired" due to the demands of those who wish to retain the supposed purity of an exclusively male-imaged God, male-dominated church, and male-articulated dogma, liturgy, and theology. Some churches withheld funds from their denomination as a means of blackmail or coercion. It is the 20th century's version of witch hunts. This writer herself was charged by some members of her congregation with heresy, paganism and perversion after attending the conference, resulting in having to leave my pulpit. A top Presbyterian woman executive on the conference's planning committee was forced to resign.

The irony of such behavior is that my faith tradition -- Presbyterian (or Reformed) — has a commitment to inclusive language, ecumenical involvement, and experimental forms of liturgical expression. More than that, it is guided by the principle *ecclesia reformata semper reformanda* (the church reformed always reforming). Because of this continuing reform aspect of faith and life within my tradition, we have accepted ten creeds to guide us over the centuries of spiritual and faith development. One of them is the Confession of 1967, which attempted to address the heresy of racism. Wonderfully, it also addresses the heresies of sexism and tribalism (such as Nazism or any branch of Christendom which claims unique and exclusive "correctness" and salvation).It also prophetically addresses the contemporary heresies of popular religion, exclusivism, and fundamentalism by affirming the mystical, inexpressible nature of the holy and a spirit of inclusiveness, compassion, and nonjudgmentalism:

> *The church comes under the judgment of God and invites rejection by (humans) when it fails to lead men and women into the full meaning of life together, or withholds the compassion of Christ from those caught in the moral confusion of our time ...*
>
> *The church gathers ... to be tested, renewed, and reformed, and to speak and act in the world's affairs as may be appropriate to the needs of the time ...*
>
> *Every church order must be open to such reformation as may be required to make it a more effective instrument of the mission of reconciliation ...*
>
> *The Christian finds parallels between other religions and his/her own and must approach all religions with openness and respect. Repeatedly God has used the insight of non-Christians to challenge the church to renewal ...*
>
> *Congregations, individuals, or groups of Christians who exclude, dominate, or patronize their fellow men (sic), however subtly, resist the Spirit of God and bring contempt on the faith which they profess...*
>
> (Quotes from "The Confession of 1967"
The Presbyterian Church, U.S.A.)

A further irony is that an unofficial Presbyterian group called "The Presbyterian Lay Committee" and its publication, *The Presbyterian Layman*, are the major entities behind the witch hunts within the Presbyterian Church U.S.A. They came into existence in the mid-60's in order to defy and attempt to overthrow the denomination's acceptance of "The Confession of 1967"! Now they fight feminism in all its forms, and seek the renouncing of "The Confession of 1967". I'm proud to say that I was earning some pocket money as Dr. Edgar A. Dowey's secretary while I was a student at Princeton Theological Seminary in 1964 when he was writing the initial drafts of the confession.

Why is there so much resistance to women in the church attempting to use feminine language in relationship to God? I am convinced that the root of the resistance lies partly in a biblical literalism that is selective and exclusive. It is a biblical literalism that feels comfortable with racism, sexism, judgmentalism and exclusivism. Its misogyny is supported by antifemale scripture texts (usually Pauline), ignoring completely Jesus' feminism. (See Leonard Swidler's *"Jesus Was A Feminist"* in the 1971 Catholic World, and Rachel Conrad Wahlberg's *Jesus According To A Woman*, New York: Paulist Press, 1975.) I also believe it lies in a reactionary determination to retain patriarchal sway at all costs-- even their souls.

Despite the Pope's attempt in 1994 to silence Roman Catholic women from even talking about women's ordination as priests, women will not be silenced. It is yet another irony that some of the most outspoken of feminist theologians are our Roman Catholic sisters, and some of the most courageous and risk-taking publishers are Roman Catholic presses.

The women at the "Re-Imagining" conference in Minneapolis, perhaps foreseeing future backlash and vindictiveness against such "uppity" women, nevertheless articulated a strong commitment to stay within the church. They were no more heretics for calling God "Sophia" than people in the pews who sing of God as "Rock of Ages." They were no more worshipping a pagan goddess than the latter are worshipping a rock. It is the biblical literalists (fundamentalists and many charismatics) who make such accusations and seek reprisals against those who do not duplicate their own brand of religion. Oddly, it is the same biblical literalists who promote in our times an early heresy of there being two gods-- God and the Devil-- at war for the world. Clearly they identify feminists (and homosexuals) with the devil ...

If the women at the "Re-Imagining" conference, showing love and inclusion for their lesbian sisters, is not what Jesus taught us in the parable of the Good Samaritan, what is it? If embracing the truths found in other world religions is not being inclusive of all God's children ("not of this fold," in Jesus' words), as we are clearly instructed to be, why isn't it? If questioning old theories of the atonement helps us put an end to violence, assassinations, crucifixions and executions, isn't that a GOOD thing? Wasn't Jesus himself questioning the idea of a sacrificial atonement when he upset the money changers' tables and insisted that he was the Lamb of God and no more sacrifices were necessary?

The Presbyterian 1994 General Assembly voted that clergy should not "bless homosexual unions." Are only heterosexual unions (50% of which end in divorce, and approximately a third of which experience family violence and incest) to be blessed? Should clergy bless any union? As the priest in the movie "The Mission" stated so aptly, without God's blessing, ours is meaningless, and with God's blessing, ours is unnecessary. So why single out homosexual unions to curse? Jesus never allowed or sanctioned such discrimination. How can we justify it? (Will they also not allow us to bless a mass murderer about to be executed in the electric chair?)

Perhaps another cause of reactions against the "Re-Imagining" conference was simply a desire to keep women in their place -- a place of silence and submission. After all, this antiwoman bias can be found throughout all cultures and societies, and it has long been rationalized and justified by institutional religion, despite the fact that Jesus never practiced nor recommended it. Elizabeth Dodson Gray's remarkable Sunday School Manifesto: *In The Image of Her* (Wellesley, MS: Roundtable Press,1994), after describing the centuries of woman hatred and oppression within the church, shows how women have nonetheless played a major role in the creation and maintenance of the church throughout its history, but especially in its earliest beginnings.

In addition, Rachel Conrad Wahlberg's *Jesus According To A Woman* outlines how again and again Jesus chose women to be the hearers and doers of the Gospel. She reinterprets nine of Jesus' encounters with women (and parables involving women) to show how committed Jesus was to the full humanity of women. (No wonder that those who do not share this commitment also tend to lag in their commitment to the full humanity of Jesus!) Gray shows how it was Mary Magdalene who was sent to tell the others about the resurrection, and that "had it not been for these women's faithfulness, there would not be an Easter morning account of the resurrection, since the male disciples had all run away and did not come to the tomb." (p. 32)

Sermons preached over the centuries about the presentation of the infant Jesus at the temple failed to acknowledge that it was Anna, the old prophetess of the temple where Jesus was brought, who was the first to claim him as the Messiah and proclaim him as such to others (Luke 2: 36-38). Gray documents how Jesus talked theology with the woman at the well, whose reaction was to become the first evangelist (John 4: 5-30). He encouraged Mary to leave Martha in the kitchen and join the men in theological debate (Luke 10: 38-42). Christine Marie Smith preached on the Canaanite woman at the "Re-Imagining" Conference, who helped convince Jesus to redefine his mission to take the Gospel to the world and not just to the Jews. Jesus affirmed women as more than just receptacles for semen or instruments of childbearing, but as hearers and doers of the word, as prophets, priestesses, missionaries, theologians and disciples.

Although the Roman Catholic, Greek and Russian Orthodox Churches refuse to ordain women, they have a long history dating back to the third and fourth centuries of veneration of Mary. Saints Justin and Ireneus, Epiphanius, Augustine, Anselm, Thomas, and Louis de Montfort, as well as Origen, attested to Mary's divine role as Mother of God and Mother of humankind. (See Patrick Gaffney, S.M.M., *Mary's Spiritual Maternity,* Bay Shore, N.Y.: Montfort Publications, 1976.) Contemporary feminist speculations about Mary's role as co-creator, co-redeemer, and even silent partner in the Trinity, are nothing new.

Even sin, Rachel Conrad Wahlberg insists, must be redefined from a woman's point of view as well as men's. To identify sin with pride, lust and aggressiveness, women writers are suggesting, is to indicate what men feel guilty about, not women. Women, like blacks, have been cautioned to hold back, be subject, suffer quietly in this world, do menial jobs. Thus, women's sin is to be self-denying, self-demeaning, reluctant to admit strength and God given creativity and potential. (p. 10)

This idea of sin, from a woman's point of view, is even suggested by the original Greek noun, *amartia*, that is most commonly translated in the New Testament as "sin". Take away the "a" at the beginning (the Greek way of making a negative out of a positive is by placing an "a" at the beginning), change the noun to a verb, and you get *martureo*, from which we get the English word "martyr". Its translations include "to speak up or speak out, to bear witness, to give testimony or make a report." To sin, therefore, is to remain silent, deny being a witness, refuse to testify to the atrocities or the miracles around you.

In a collection of poems I edited titled *Family Violence: Poems On The Pathology* (La Jolla, CA: Moonlight Publications, 1982), I explain this concept of sin in the Introduction, urging women and children who have been abused to speak up, speak out, and speak for an end to the violence. Only by their speaking can this critical social tragedy be stopped. The book received a grant to be distributed to every shelter for battered women and children in the country where it is used as a resource for group therapy. Scores of women have written me, telling me how important it was for them to learn to break out of their silence, to give speech to the horror of their lives, and by speaking of it, to move past it to a new healing and peaceful place.

Elizabeth Dodson Gray writes: "Feminists have concluded that Christianity's contempt for women and their bodies has been an essential backdrop legitimating the violence against women." Tracing the history of violence against women, feminist writers point out the witch hunts, the crusades, war and rape, and countless assaults of incest, child abuse, wife-beating and murder. Gray underlines that "the perpetrators are not just individual males who are violent. It is the entire tradition which is culpable of doing structural, theological violence to women... You cannot have a children-friendly tradition until you have a woman-respecting tradition. When Christian theology, ritual, and practices denigrate and abuse their mothers, it hurts children-- just as it hurts children to watch battering husbands beating their mothers."

Women must not remain silent. We must speak out. Not to do so is sin. To do so is righteousness, even if our speaking out is a cry of pain and outrage, or a cry of accusation against our enemies, like the cries of the prophets. Our speech is intended to stop the atrocities, to end the violations and oppressions, not to hurt the oppressors.

Brueggemann explains that "it is Israel's 'cry of absence' that makes God's speech of presence possible" and

> *Where there is no compelling speech, where there is no cry of absence and oracle of presence, life withers, persons shrivel, and community becomes impossible. Without this speech we grieve hopelessly and unaltered in our silence, not understanding what is happening to us, for we do not know that we must speak and listen and answer in order to live. (p. 65)*

We cannot and must not be silenced. It would be a sin. Rachel Conrad Wahlberg says that "to balance nineteen centuries of Christian dogma interpreted from the male point of view, women writers, professors and theologians are needed to balance out negative attitudes concerning women which pervade major Christian thinkers from Paul to Augustine to the present." (p. 10) One of the ways we are doing this is biblical revisioning. Jewish poet and feminist theologian Alicia Ostriker is in the forefront of such endeavors. The poems in this book do precisely that.

One of the most playful pastimes of feminist writers and theologians is to break the chains and shackles that bind men and women. Some of those chains have been wrought over the centuries by the church, under the thrall of men. With our new vision of mutuality, partnership, reciprocity, and responsibility, both men and women are liberated and energized into recreating the kind of world that has nothing to do with the fiefdoms and dominance/submission paradigms. It is a world where the greatest power is love and respect, not a power over, but a power with, an empowerment of. Wahlberg says,

> *If we are not all liberated in Christ, then no one is liberated. It is imperative that all free-spirited women and men insist that the church carry out its true freedom in the Gospel by dispelling at all levels --and in all its segments, doctrine, hierarchies, interpretation and preaching -- any vestige of discrimination against any group of people. (pp. 11-12)*

Elizabeth Dodson Gray agrees:

> *What I am calling for is another Reformation of Christendom freeing us this time not from the power of the pope and priest but from the power of patriarchal males whatever their position. To urge this is to challenge nearly all of our traditions, and it is an awesome challenge... Feminism is God's call to us, in this generation, to open up to radical change so that our tradition may be true again to Jesus, and become life-affirming for all. (p. 74)*

This book is a collection of paintings and poems that attempt to create even more new images and metaphors for understanding God and our relationship with God. A few of the poems herein have already been judged heretical or blasphemous by some. (I was fired from leadership at a 1993 church women's retreat because the organizer read my "Lot" poems and disliked them!) That's because they were taken literally. Even the Bible, taken literally, would be unacceptable to most, or would be mostly unacceptable. Show Picasso's "Guernica" to ten people. Let them study it at length. Ask them what it means or says to them. You'll get ten different responses. Each are true; each are false. THIS IS OK!

If these paintings of the stations of the Via Dolorosa don't conjure in your mind the same images they did in the painter or in the poems accompanying them, that's OK! Open your mind to the revelations and teachings of God's Spirit today. Allow God's wisdom to assist you in your discernments. This is what the poem herein titled "Sophia Mandala" seeks.

When I asked Dr. Will Carl, my homiletics professor at Phillips Graduate Seminary, how could I be so arrogant as to do my own translation of Scripture in my sermons or poems, he responded, "Mary, not only is it OK; it's necessary. As a minister called by God and trained by others similarly called, it is your responsibility to do it."

Our journey through life can be so much richer, so much easier, if we will open our eyes and hearts wider, reach our arms out broader, and seek insights even from our supposed enemies. We must never give up, or be silenced. As one poem herein states: "the only cardinal sin is silence, and the only mortal sin is despair."

Now, journey on.

The Pathway

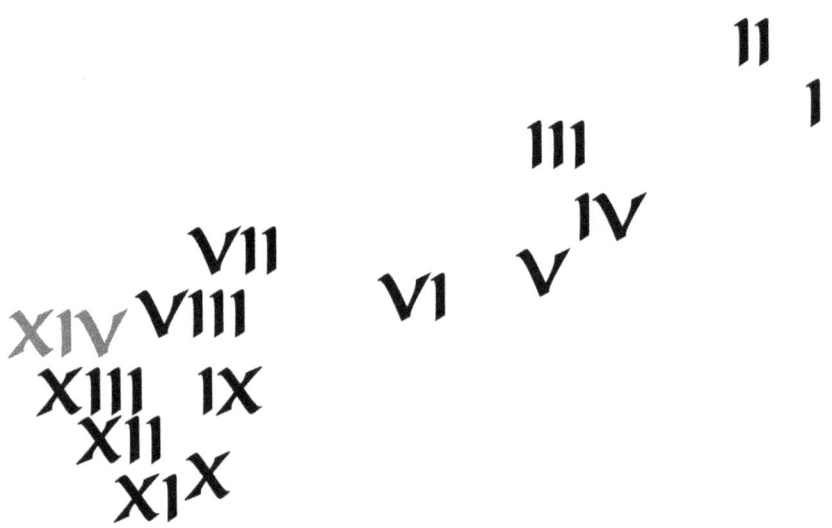

The Stations of the Cross

Station One: The Verdict

Who has believed what we have heard? And to whom has the arm of the Lord been revealed? For he grew up before him like a young plant, and like a root out of dry ground; he had no form or majesty that we should look at him, nothing in his appearance that we should desire him. He was despised and rejected by others: a man of suffering and acquainted with infirmity; and as one from whom others hide their faces he was despised, and we held him of no account.

Surely he has borne our infirmities and carried our diseases, yet we accounted him stricken, struck down by God, and afflicted. But he was wounded for our transgressions, crushed for our iniquities; upon him was the punishment that made us whole, and by his bruises we are healed.

All we like sheep have gone astray; we have all turned to his own way; and the Lord has laid on him the iniquity of us all. He was oppressed, and he was afflicted, yet he did not open his mouth; like a lamb that is led to the slaughter, and like a sheep that before its shearers is silent, so he did not open his mouth.

By a perversion of justice he was taken way. Who could have imagined his future? For he was cut off from the land of the living, stricken for the transgressions of my people. They made his grave with the wicked and his tomb with the rich, although he had done no violence, and there was no deceit in his mouth.

Yet it was the will of the Lord to crush him with pain. When you make his life an offering for sin, he shall see his offspring, and shall prolong his days; through him the will of the Lord shall prosper. Out of his anguish he shall see light; he shall find satisfaction through his knowledge. The righteous one, my servant, shall make many righteous, and he shall bear their iniquities. Therefore I will allot him a portion with the great, and he shall divide the spoil with the strong; because he poured out himself to death, and was numbered with the transgressors; yet he bore the sin of many, and made intercession for the transgressors. Isaiah 53

Then Pilate took Jesus and had him flogged. And the soldiers wove a crown of thorns and put it on his head, and they dressed him in a purple robe. They kept coming up to him, saying, "Hail, King of the Jews!" and striking him on the face. Pilate went out again, and said to them, "Behold, I am bringing him out to you to let you know that I find no case against him." So Jesus came out, wearing the crown of thorns and the purple robe. Pilate said to them, "Here is the man!" When the chief priests and the police saw him, they shouted, "Crucify him, crucify him!"

Pilate said to them, "Take him yourselves and crucify him. I find no case against him." The Jews answered him, "We have a law, and according to that law he ought to die, because he has claimed to be the Son of God."

Station I Continued...

When Pilate heard this, he was more afraid than ever. He entered his headquarters again and asked Jesus, "Where are you from?" But Jesus gave him no answer. Pilate therefore said to him, "Do you refuse to speak to me? Do you not know that I have power to release you, and power to crucify you?" Jesus answered him, "You would have no power over me unless it had been given you from above; therefore the one who handed me over to you is guilty of the greater sin."

From then on Pilate tried to release him, but the Jews cried out, "If you release this man, you are no friend of the emperor. Everyone who claims to be a king sets himself against the emperor."

When Pilate heard these words, he brought Jesus outside and sat on the judge's bench at a place called The Stone Pavement, or in Hebrew, Gabbatha. Now it was the day of preparation for the Passover; and it was about noon. He said to the Jews, "Here is your King!" They cried out, "Away with him, Away with him, Crucify him!" Pilate asked them, "Shall I crucify your King?" The chief priests answered, "We have no king but the emperor." Then he handed him over to them to be crucified.

So they took Jesus, and carrying the cross by himself, he went out to what is called The Place of the Skull, which in Hebrew is called Golgotha. There they crucified him...

John 19:1 -18a

(See also Mark 15:1 - 20; Matthew 24:11 - 31 and Luke 23:1 - 25 for other descriptions of these events.)

The Verdict

Station One is in fact a playground
in a Muslim boys school,
built by the Turks.

The view in the painting is looking East. ...
The area is a bit larger than a basketball court.

The Via Dolorosa begins just outside this courtyard.
It is not yet a thoroughfare.

Two small cars might have difficulty passing each other.
A truck would have to climb the sidewalk to let a car pass.
You are about to take the first step on the Way of Sorrows.

Anita Roper writes that the *Stations* "begin with the sentence of death all humans face (Sta.1) and move to the fullness of life we are able to choose by showing how absolutely God accepted the human condition in Jesus Christ." She shows 'the way' as the ability to say yes to life, courage to believe God dwells among us as one of us, ability to give and accept help, the relational nature of love, and faith in the meaningfulness and purpose of suffering.

(*The Fifteenth Station*. New York, Herder & Herder, 1967)

Step One in the Twelve-Step Program of Alcoholics Anonymous (AA) is where we admit we are powerless over our separation from God -- our addictions -- and our lives have become unmanageable.

"Bare"ing the Sins of the Fathers
Bearing the Sins of the Fathers

> *"Human experience is the starting point*
> *and the ending point of the hermeneutical circle."*
> Rosemary Radford Ruether

1. This is how it begins:
   whip on flesh, flesh on bone,
   bone in desert dry and distant.
   > *("Dem bones, dem bones gwine rise agin...")*
   All beginnings require some baptism in blood and water,
   so the first step
   is a cleansing, a circumcision of the soul.
   > *("Dem bones, dem bones gwine rise agin...")*
   It all revolves around how you think about the body.
   Questions of spirit and matter.
   > *("Dem bones, dem bones gwine rise agin...")*
   Thomas Mann's priest said
   you cannot experience the world without the body, the flesh.
   > *("Now hear de word of de Lawd.")*

2. One scourge for Adam, blaming Eve,
   eating the apple of seduction, of knowledge
   that lost the world its innocence.
   > *("De toe bone connected to de foot bone.")*
   This scar marks the murderer Cain
   who killed his brother Abel; did exile
   East of Eden put an end to fratricide?
   > *("De foot bone connected to de ankle bone.")*
   This bloody rainbow's arc across his back
   recalls the curse of Noah on his sons
   for seeing their drunken father naked.
   > *("De ankle bone connected to de shin bone.")*
   These sword wounds in the side
   are Lot's, for every wife unnamed, neglected,
   every daughter molested.
   > *("Now hear de word of de Lawd.")*

3. The weight of Abraham's sins requires
a special flagellation; his willingness
to sacrifice sons to serve self.
   ("De shin bone connected to de knee bone.")
For Ishmael, his firstborn son, deserted,
castaway Jew, wandering these centuries
the desert sands of paternal denial, fraternal hatred.
   ("De knee bone connected to de thigh bone")
For Hagar, handmaiden, used to birth his child
both abandoned in the shifting dunes of Arabia
destined to call her god Allah.
   ("De thigh bone connected to de hip bone.")
For beautiful Sarah, sold to Pharoah
and kings for Abraham's safety and wealth;
for Keturah, and all the buried wives.
   ("Now hear de word of de Lawd.")

4. "Imago Dei" must mean, if nothing else,
that God put all the lessons of life
where we could learn them from our bodies.
   ("De hip bone connected to de back bone.")
That pain causes us to take our fingers
out of the fire. That relationships
effect our health, comprise our wealth.
   ("De back bone connected to de rib bone.")
That true pain is never just physiological;
that deepest suffering is in mind and spirit;
that the only real dying is not to celebrate the living.
   ("De rib bone connected to de shoulder bone.")

5. That overcrowded lemmings commit suicide;
rats don't reproduce;
That some fish in the presence of enemies
become enlarged and difficult to eat.
   ("De shoulder bone connected to de neck bone.")
That certain squid ejaculate their guts
to escape their predators; that beaten wives
beat children who torture puppies and kittens
   ("De neck bone connected to de head bone.")
That all wars, throughout all time, are caused by this:
one person denying another person
the singular designation "Child of God".
   (Now hear de word of de Lawd.)
(This is how it begins:
in the presence of the Holy we are first of all silent.
When finally able to speak,

confession tumbles out
like blood from deep wounds.
Purged, we turn like sunflowers
toward the sun, grateful
for this day, this night.
There is this God who suffers yet lives,
despairs yet loves, bleeds the blood
that is living water for the world.)
              Now hear the Word of the Lord.

Ecce Homo

> "Are you a man or a mouse?
> Yes I am, yes I am."
> -- Dick Bakken

> "Dear Jesus in whose life I see
> all that I would but fail to be.
> --Hymn

Take a look at yourself.
Take a real long, real good
    look at yourself.
Whaddaya see?
Are you "only human"
    or also holy?
Who do you say that you are?
    Who do you say that he is?
Surely if any life is to be redeemed
    it will only be
by being fully human, fully divine,
    like him.

Ecce Homo - Latin for "behold the man" or "look at the person or being."

STATION TWO: JESUS TAKES UP THE CROSS

After mocking him, they stripped him of the robe and put his own clothes on him. Then they led him away to crucify him.

Matthew 27:31

After mocking him, they stripped him of the purple cloak, and put his own clothes on him. Then they led him out to crucify him.

Mark 15:20

So Pilate gave his verdict that their demand should be granted. He released the man they asked for, the one who had been put in prison for insurrection and murder, and he handed Jesus over as they wished ... Two others also, who were criminals, were led away to be put to death with him.

Luke 23:24,25 and 32.

Then Jesus told his disciples. "If any want to become my followers, let them deny themselves and take up their cross and follow me. For those who want to save their life will lose it, and those who lose their life for my sake will find it."

Matthew 16:24-25

JESUS TAKES UP THE CROSS

We cross the street
and enter a small, tree-shaded park
about the size of the Ralph Bunche Memorial Park
in New York City.

Off this courtyard are two chapels.
One is the Chapel of the Flagellation,
which was built in medieval times and restored in 1929.

Opposite is the Church of the Condemnation of Christ
and the Imposition of the Cross.

Inside the chapels are ornate mosaics and frescoes
depicting Jesus taking up the cross.

This ancient fragment of a column, still standing,
stark and alone, shows how the place feels.

It is Step Two of the AA Twelve-Step Program where we come to believe that there is a power greater than ours available to us, which can restore us to wholeness and sanity. (We will refer to that greater power as God, however the reader may understand that power. For example, it could be "the force" -- of nature or law or whatever -- or simply the will/power of the larger community, or the church, or the tribal elders, or the family.)

TAKING UP THE CROSS
(For Father Dan Berrigan, S. J., who wrote,
"The ideogram is of a man standing by his word.")

"My life is the poem I would have writ were it not for the constant living of it."
--HenryDavid Thoreau

1. RALPH BUNCHE *(1904- 1971)*
From the streets of Detroit, through the ivy halls of the academy, to the Congo rain forests and the Yemen desert, this black American worked to unite nations and peoples. Leading the United Nations' Palestine Commission in 1949, he helped forge the armistice between Arab and Jew. Nobel prized his peacemaking in 1950. No American teenager will kill another teenager for a pair of Ralph Bunche sneakers.

2. BEN LINDNER *(1959-1987)*
This young Jewish man from Washington took an engineering degree, a unicycle and a clown costume to Nicaragua to see how he might help the Sandinistas rebuild their country. He used the first to help build a dam upcountry, the unicycle and clown costume to charm children from the hills into the local clinic for their inoculations. On a clinic wall in Managua is a plaque honoring him; just outside is a park and children's playground named after him. He carried a gun for protection from the Contras, but never used it. When they killed him, with arms from the U.S.A., George Bush said he had asked for it.

3. THE MISSION
In this remarkable movie, one priest takes up the crucifix and stands singing and praying with the South American native people as they are gunned down by the European colonists. Another priest takes up a musket and dies fighting with the people.
Each human chooses their own cross.
Each of these lives is a poem.

Woman Rising
or
The Poet As An Agent For Social Change

"Witness the binding of the feet. Bonsai."
--Terry Hauptman

She rises from the lake, dripping water
like wax from a penitent's candle.
Her feet send tendrils rootlike green
in all directions, roots that bind,
that heal, as lasers wrapping sound to sight.

Inside the cave, beneath the river bottom,
past the sonic boom into the inner ear
the sound of much growing
aches into the nerve.
This is our only given, the primal absolute;
it echoes from her lips of blue/black bruise,
going on:

"Change," she whispers
to the north of ice and fear, her flesh trembling.

"Change," she cries
to the south of fire and pain, her heart exploding.

"Change," she sobs
to the west of darkness and grief, her belly quaking.

"Change," she screams
to the east of dawn and love, her arms embracing.

Amartia

"I often feel we are sinning not to be conscious of the terrible suffering of the whole earth and its flesh, crying, its need so great.

"Meridel LeSueur, 1993

In the journey of my life there are four women.
Mother, sister, daughter, and my work.
When I move into them and out of them I am whole,
carrying them with me. Though they may stare
baffled at each other and at me
we know the common thread, communal dance.
They shrug and swoon with me, shaking skirts and fists,
weeping and weaving, gnawing and knowing.
The fathers are absent; brothers killed in wars.
Study the scars and the scat; see there the disease
that accompanies the endless struggle for power and riches.
Behind our brothers' eyes is the torn veil of sight
that longs to look in another's face.
The women are saying clearly: desist from conquests.
The women say plainly: no more whores or warriors,
no more using, abusing, exploiting, or owning.
Now is the time for a new sharing.
The sleeping dog is dying; do not just let it lie.
Lift it in your arms and hold it.
Hear the children calling for us to choose them,
hear them coming to choose us, to call us to life.
There will be a new gathering, a new congress
of peoples whose flag will be the bluest sky,
the clearest waters; whose code will be the righteous
trumpet of joy, temple of peace. In their song
will be a rising of wings, a deep sighing.
We can start where we are, this step, this day.
We can begin the new dances found in each other's feet.
We can see new things to do with our hands, our voices,
we can build a world together where
the only cardinal sin is silence,
the only mortal sin is despair.

Amartia: In the New Testament, the Greek word *matureo* (from which we get the English "martyr") is a verb which means "to speak out or speak up, to protest, to bear witness or give testimony." By putting an a in front of it and changing it to a noun, it becomes *amartia*, which is commonly translated throughout the New Testament as "sin". In short, the Greek understanding of sin was to remain silent: to refuse to advocate for justice or protest against injustices, to testify or bear witness to the atrocities.

Station Three: Jesus Falls for the First Time

There is no specific biblical text indicating that Jesus fell, although there is much to suggest it. For example: "The arrogant have hidden a trap for me, and with cords they have spread a net; along the road they have set snares for me." (Psalm 140:5)

The three texts that mention Simon of Cyrene being required to help Jesus carry the cross (Matthew 27:32; Mark 12:21; Luke 23:26 -- see Station V) suggest that Jesus may have fallen and was in need of help.

It is reasonable to assume that in his weakened condition, having been beaten severely, he struggled under the weight of the cross (which was probably about 75 pounds).

JESUS FALLS FOR THE FIRST TIME

Halfway up the block from Station II,
the Via Dolorosa makes a little dogleg turn to the left.

Station III is marked by a doorway behind a wrought-iron gate.
Here, as all over Jerusalem, there is evidence of graffiti.
Typically one group paints political slogans at night
and the next day the opposition comes with black paint
and obliterates them.
The result is abstract images.
Everywhere you see pictures Franz Kline would envy.

The building here is currently a church and school
administered by the Armenian Catholic Church.
Prior to this, the building was a Turkish bath.

Are these the true spots?
I met a nun at this Station who was a sort of caretaker.
She volunteered: "You know, no one can be sure
if these were the actual stones Jesus trod,
but we accept the site as holy because of the
veneration of the millions of pilgrims
who have believed it to be so."
This "retro-sanctification" seems good enough for me.

In fact, there is reasonable evidence — a hill which actually looks like a skull near a site with many early rock-hewn tombs — that might suggest the whole path is about a half a mile too far south. Here, there, elsewhere...it makes no matter; the important thing is, God visits us and walks with us.

It is at Step Three of the AA program where we make a decision to turn our wills and lives over to a superior being or force — God, as we understand God to be. This is commonly called "the leap of faith" — that trusting acknowledgment that we are not able to do it alone.

FIRST FALL

Genesis 1, 2 and 3

It's not that we deny biting the apple.
It's just that we don't feel we should have
to apologize for seeking knowledge.
That first taste of freedom was delicious
and now we can't live without it. So
out we go, banished from Eden,
but given a cosmos to wander. Freedom,
yes. But there is a price to pay.
To care for earth and all that's in it! So much
it takes each one of us, each succeeding
generation, endlessly, tilling the fields with care,
never poisoning the air or polluting the streams.
And the animals — ants and antelopes, creeping,
crawling, leaping, flying, dear God
and if we don't do it, we'll all die!

SYZYGY

I want to believe
that the world is somehow
 sort of
God created
that there is a moral definition
of our lives
some kind of sun-beam'd
sacred design
and direction
where once each regulated time period
the planets line up in order
across the black holes of space
and all our ancestors
peer down the sights of time
and know the future is safe
in our hands.

syz - y - gy From Greek literature; state of being yoked together; unity; the nearly straight line configuration of three celestial bodies (as the sun, moon and earth during a solar or lunar eclipse) in a gravitational system; a group of two coupled feet in Greek or Latin prosody; a pair of correlatives, opposites, or otherwise related things; a pair of Gnostic aeons male and female (i.e. the syzygy of humankind and church). In 1987 the earth experienced a syzygy of all the planets in our solar system being aligned in a row.

Our Mother's Body Is The Earth

Our mother's body is the earth,
her aura is the air, her spirit
is in the middle, round like an egg,
and she contains all good things in herself,
like a honeycomb.
She squats and the rivers flow;
her breasts are the hills,
her nipples the trees.
Her breath scatters leaves
on the shifting sands of her belly,
and her knees roll out caverns and canyons below.
Her menses make the ocean floor shift,
and tidal waves proclaim her pain.
When we, her children, return to her,
on knee, in ash or in dust,
her flesh is scarred with accepting us back
and her intestines growl at our death.
Mountains erupt with her agony
and pour us back into the sea
to hiss and spume her orgasm.

The Luxury Of Guilt and Grief
(For Carolyn Forche')

There was a woman who cried
forgive me God for I have
sinned and am heartily
ashamed. I am unable to sleep
with a man and my thoughts
keep tapping on the curbstone
of defeat. My floors
are covered with newspapers
and my scalp is crusted
with dirt. On this trip
my wheels betrayed a field mouse
and two turtles stayed
up-ended on the road of no time
to stop. Forgive me for the woman
in my yard who calls and moves away,
the plant that withers without water,
the food left wasted on the table.

Forgive me because
we have become a nation
that paves the Garden of Eden
for profit and takes music
out of the schools, that pays
athletes more than teachers and
movie stars more than single moms,
where children kill for sneakers
and churches preach prosperity.

Forgive me for wallowing
in guilt and isolating in grief
when there is so much
so much
work to do.

Station Four: Jesus Encounters His Mother Mary

When Jesus saw his mother, and the disciple whom he loved standing beside her, he said to his mother, "Woman, here is your son." Then he said to the disciple, "Here is your mother." And from that hour the disciple took her into his own home.

John 19:26- 27

Jesus Encounters His Mother Mary

A few more steps down the road,
around the corner, is a side entrance
to the same Armenian church building.

Over the door is a bas relief sculpture
illuminating the encounter of Jesus with his mother Mary.

Tradition says that "Mary, meeting her Son bearing His cross, fell under the weight of her anguish. Upon the place of this awful meeting a chapel was raised which took the name of St. Mary of the Spasm." (Thomas L. Kinkead and Michael Augustine, Editors, *Catholic Ceremonies*. New York: Benzinger Bros., 1896, p. 205.)

At AA's Step Four we stop to make a searching and fearless moral inventory of ourselves.

ANNUNCIATION

Luke 1:26-38

When the angel announced I would bear him,
my innocence agreed, though the thought of it
terrified me. I could have been stoned
to death. But now the years
turn amniotic bliss to tears; eternally
we bear, earth's nameless mothers,
sisters, daughters, swollen breasts
of our longing for life and love.
Let me not say in my own despair and grief,
"I wish he had never been born."
Such a song is the saddest song
ever to be sung. And yet a sadder still
"I refuse to bring children into such a world."
I have one truth: the truth all mothers have:
I know the father's name.
And with this one small truth
I say
each child is a child of God.
Let the fathers own their own creations,
own their need for us, their use of us,
even God.

REBEKAH'S POEM

Genesis 27

I don't feel good about
deceiving Issac.
I feel even worse
disinheriting Esau.
But it's time someone started
a new paradigm:
henceforth the Number One Son
is the gentle one, the tender one,
the one who honors the mother!

Station Five: Simon of Cyrene Helps Carry The Cross

As they went out, they came upon a man from Cyrene named Simon; they compelled this man to carry his cross.

Matthew 27:32

They compelled a passer-by, who was coming in from the country, to carry his cross; it was Simon of Cyrene, the father of Alexander and Rufus.

Mark 15:21

As they led him away, they seized a man, Simon of Cyrene, who was coming in from the country, and laid the cross on him, and made him carry it behind Jesus.

Luke 23:26

Simon of Cyrene Helps Carry The Cross

The road makes another quick turn,
and at this corner
is the door to a Franciscan chapel built in 1895.

The "Stations of the Cross"
were fostered by the Franciscans,
who were guardians of the holy places in Jerusalem,
"as a simulation of the pilgrimage procession
along the Via Dolorosa",
the traditional route taken by Jesus
on the way to his Crucifixion.

The number of stations have varied throughout the centuries, but fourteen are now authorized. "Q.C.J. Metford, *Dictionary of Christian Lore and legend*. London: Thames & Hudson, Ltd., 1983, p. 232.)

Step Five for AA is where we admit to God (as we understand God), to ourselves, and to at least one other person the exact nature of our wrongs and shortcomings.

Help
(For all who have been convicted)

> " 'He is a sinner' you are pleased to say.
> Then love him for the sake of Christ, I pray.
> If on His gracious words you place your trust,
> 'I came to call the sinners, not the just/
> Second his call; which if you will not do,
> You'll be the greater sinner of the two."
> —John Byrom, 18th century poet

Convict, I, with metal heart and hand
stand surly, snarling, cuffed at Heaven's Door,
this door but just one more behind a million doors
each marked with gold and promises anew
if I but enter through, and entering,
fall back on self and sin, each time
a new indictment, new despair.

But then, my cellmate of a sudden there,
her hair all caked with blood, her eyes
aflame with pain, her fractured legs
strain bravely with each step, no petty
punishment endured, no temporary rest secured
for dark betrayals of her friends; no,
once she went for me before the board
and thereby lowered sentencing; stands now
with sweat on brow, appealing,
burden groaning, last fandango flopground
looming, dragging, straining,
lifting load across the threshold here.

But reaching out to lift with her,
our burdens disappear! No mere
illusion this! My heart explodes
and cloud-tongue tremble of the galaxies
sing music in my ear!

Station Six: The Woman Wipes His Bloody Brow

There is nothing in biblical literature to suggest that a woman in the crowd wiped blood from the brow of Jesus during his travail up the hill toward Golgotha.

In extracanonical literature, however, dating back to the second and third centuries, specifically in a late Latin insertion into the Gospel of Nicodemus, the story is told how "Jesus stumbles under the weight of his cross on the way to his Crucifixion, and a woman stepped out of the crowd and wiped the sweat from his face. After he had moved on, she found that his features were imprinted on the handkerchief, cloth or veil which she had used. This relic has been in Rome since the 8th century. It is now in a chapel in the crypt of St. Peter's." Q.C.J. Metford, *Dictionary of Christian Lore and Legend*. London: Thames & Hudson, Ltd., 1983, p. 252.)

Metford's dictionary goes on to say that some have thought, on the authority of the original text of the Gospel of Nicodemus, that this woman who was later canonized as St. Veronica was in fact the woman with the issue of blood, named in that book as "Berenike". (Metford, *Dictionary*, p. 252). The name Veronica, like Berenike, comes from the Latin *vera* (true) and *icon* (image), relating to the "true image" of Jesus on the cloth.

In Caryll Houselander's meditations on Christ's journey, she stages a drama that shows us the passion itself reflected or even relived in all human suffering. She says "we can no longer be detached voyeurs or spectators of the world's griefs and despairs, but are required to be the world's Veronicas and Jesuses, suffering in solidarity with it and dying for it. Every time we wipe away the tears of the world's ravages we will find the same image Veronica did on our handkerchiefs." (Caryll Houselander, *The Way of the Cross*. New York: Sheed & Ward, 1955, flyleaf comment.)

The Woman Wipes His Bloody Brow

Now we are going more sharply up a hill
on our way to the top — Calvary.

As a hill, it is about as steep as a 30-degree incline.
Nowadays, the street is quite busy at this point
with tiny shops, bakeries,
fruit and vegetable stands, jewelers and hawkers
trying to sell everything possible to the tourist traffic.

Most of these establishments seem to be run by Palestinians,
but there is evidence of every ancient culture:
Jewish, Greek, Coptic, Muslim, Byzantine,
intermingled in the Old City of Jerusalem.

At this site is a chapel shrine to St. Veronica,
whose house, tradition holds, once stood here.

AA's Step Six is where we are entirely ready to have God remove all our defects of character, and we are humbled as we stand before this greater power.

The Saint of the True Image
For Archbishop Oscar Romero 1917-1980)

Encased behind glass
inside the small apartment
that was his home,
near the hospital chapel in El Salvador
where the government goons gunned him down,
Archbishop Romero's blood-stained robes
attest to the atrocity and verify this verity:
the cup of wine he lifted in communion
that spilled when the shots rang out
appeared on his robe as blood.

Imago Dei
For a nun in Nicaragua

If you want to be like him, she said,
you must drink from four cups.

The first is compassion, the *sine qua non*.
If you are not moved by the dog thumping
under the car's wheels, or the seal's eyes
appealing against the clubs,
or the raped woman's shriek,
you must not lift the second cup.

The second cup is righteous anger,
the kind that overturns the tables
of the money changers; the kind
that will not abide injustice; the kind
that criticizes, analyzes, transforms.

Then follows the third soon after:
the cup of revolutionary humility.
Because we cannot do it alone.
Because we live in time and space
and both liberation and redemption
come in kairos by God's grace.

The final cup, the wine and hyssop,
the cup of solidarity,
is drunk by prophets, saints and martyrs
who wish it might be otherwise
but drink the bitter wine in the end
proclaiming, Lord,
into your hands I commend my spirit.

STATION SEVEN: JESUS FALLS A SECOND TIME

There is no explicit biblical evidence for Jesus falling (see Station III), although there is scriptural reference to his being assisted by Simon of Cyrene (see Station V).

Jesus Falls A Second Time

Another 40 yards up the hill we are at
the dark end of the street.
The high point of the hill and the crossroads
of the current Old City are here.
It is awash in people, buying, selling, going, coming,
pushing carts, guiding tourists, everyone devoted
to a material or spiritual pursuit.
A kind of "Grand Central Station."
At the top of the hill - the end of the street - is a door
which appears to go nowhere and seems to be sealed.
This door marks the gateway of the city through which
Jesus passed as he went "outside the camp" to Golgotha.
It was afterwards referred to as the Judgment Gate.

At AA's Step Seven we humbly ask God (as we understand God) to remove all our shortcomings.

THE FALL

I didn't know what mystery I sought
in my agony to know God, what apples I might
be willing to steal. Coming upon the scene,
I certainly wouldn't have seen God
in this ugly but harmless Jew fallen on the Via here.
What perverse theodicy could this be?
I must have always wanted
some stranger metamorphosis, perhaps,
than Presbyterians avowed, some magic altering
of the flesh and blood, some trembling touching
of the Grail, some mystical incantations
I could understand from taking 8th-grade Latin.
At 14 I sneaked away to the Church of St. Francis
of Assisi and Our Lady of Guadalupe, joined
the others at the altar taking wine and wafer
on my knees. I read *The Lives of the Saints*
and wore a rosary as a necklace, playing the album
"Jeanne D'Arc au Bucher" repeatedly, sobbing
every time they set her flesh aflame. I even
heard Sts. Katherine and Mary calling in my dreams,
and put St. Christopher's medal on my ankle bracelet.
To tell these truths today is like going
to a confessional, which alone could cause Calvin
to turn in his grave. And all my Scots and Irish
forebears who wagoned their way to Broken Arrow

in 1904 and set up country storefronts
all in a neat puritan row, would appeal to
John Knox for help for this aimless daughter
of the faith who was baptized at birth, reaffirmed
at 12, made her vows to follow Christ, to serve
in love this irresistible grace.
And so opened the corpus of my history
as I passively took the gospel for the truth it is
and sought the *Mysterium Tremendum* in butterfly,
song and poem. No accident that my spirit animal
is the cardinal, bright flash of red, jazzy docent
of God on my journey to profession. I know now
as I swallow faith in this Reformed tradition
that with that single claim, "he is the Christ,"
like Peter I was instantaneously petrified,
transformed into a rock. All the middle years
invoking that awe, that mystery of sealing
by the water and the Word, were spent outside
that congregation, doing all the things
that mystified me: sex and drugs and politics
and brief immersions in the ancient arts,
developing a taste for the real wine of stewardship
in the new wineskins of social change.
Somehow the coming home was all the more significant
because I had dreamed in kraals and chanted in rondovels,
had walked mean streets and prayed in kivas
no one else has even seen,
smoked sacred mushrooms of the heart
and danced with lovers like sufis on hot coals.
Rock. Stone. Stoned. Rock of Ages, cleft for me.
My scars inside,my bleeding heart the virgin's own,
my diabetes silent accuser of things I abused
my high blood pressure witness to all things that abused me.
Meridel LeSueur would write, "it all comes
in whatever you got left," and so I know
this fallen Jew, just as he knows me, this
God being who falters here, fallen on his knees,
whose Gethsemane reveals the longing not to suffer,
whose chastisement of the sleeping disciples
displays the yearning not to suffer alone,
whose cross is the transformation of all suffering
into meaningful, eternal life.   I have fallen now
into the tradition of my Scots and Presbyterian
ancestors, of caring for history,
of turning suffering and grief into ceremony, of revering blood.

STATION EIGHT: JESUS COMFORTS THE WOMEN

A great number of the people followed him, and among them were women who were beating their breasts and wailing for him. But Jesus turned to them and said, "Daughters of Jerusalem, do not weep for me, but weep for yourselves and for your children. For the days are surely coming when they will say, 'Blessed are the barren, and the wombs that never bore, and the breasts that never nursed.' Then they will begin to say to the mountains, 'Fall on us'; and to the hills, 'Cover us'. For if they do this when the wood is green, what will happen when it is dry? "

Luke 23:27 - 31

JESUS COMFORTS THE WOMEN

Station VIII is very easy to miss. It is (respectfully)
a hole in the wall....

The wall is of a Greek Orthodox convent.
The stone which is venerated
as the Station where the women were comforted,
is inscribed with the Greek letters"*NIKE*",
which means "Jesus Christ conquers."

It is also the name of a conquering Greek god.

The proprietor of the "Eighth Station Souvenir Shop"
across the way, has affixed a small banner
to a wire coat hanger
which directs your attention to the spot.

Otherwise you would miss both the Station
and his establishment.

Step Eight for AA is where we make a list of all persons we have harmed and become willing to make amends to them all.

Dinah

Genesis 34

Imagine the matriarchs mattering,
the first daughters figuring.
Then invoke Sarah, Leah, Dinah
with Abraham, Isaac, Jacob.

Our stories would be more
than tales of takings,
buyings, tradings. Our reach
would be a grab.

The lesson of history
would be well learned: that
birthright not shared
is birthright lost.

Jesus Addresses Miriam

For Alicia Ostriker -2-93

Sweet daughter of rivers and deltas
of parted reeds and swollen breasts,
if I were just God
and not also this Nazarene
      born in Bethlehem
I, Yahweh, would have come to you in the desert
of your self-discovery and drank
with you from your hidden well
like I left the tents of Abraham and Sarah
      to comfort Hagar and Ishmael.
I, Jehovah, would appear to you,
lactating like Rachel weeping
at the cries of a hungry babe
moved to action by sensed need,
      bruised reed.
I, Elohim, would have taken sand and spit
and shaped your missing fingers back
upon your hands, those busy anemone
moving in, through, across life's waters
      singing and dancing your freedom.
I, El Shaddai, would have taken this twisted tree
to part the Jordan's waters for you,
sweet freedom fighter, soul sister,
just as you parted the reeds of the Nile
      for your brother Moses.
Sister of God, I, Allah, would have danced
all night with you beneath the stars
of the desert skies, thrumming
the heartstrings of God like the timbrals
      of David and Salome.
I, Shekinah, would have kissed your leprous breasts
to bare the bleeding heart of Mary
and then announced to the Milky Way
just as I did that star-crossed day
      "behold ... your mother."

Lot's Wife

Genesis 19

We all look back
nameless women
whose future can only be worse
than the past we've at least survived.
What sin did I do
to become this saltlick
in God's wasteland?

Lot's Daughters

Genesis 19

Our father said she was turned
into a pillar of salt. We say
she died long before that, when he offered us
to expiate his enemies; when he raped us
in his drunkenness. They think we are theirs,
these fathers and these brothers
who claim to protect us, but use us
to serve their needs, protect their egos.

And so we serve, proving ourselves
by being less, turning leastness into
making the most of it. Nevertheless,
our marrow renews innocence, like our blood
renews each month, except those months
when birth is at their end.

    And so
we birth, bringing into being our own
father's sons, knowing the pain
of borning, the push of going on,
the angel wrestle as we mother and father
our new selves into being. Maybe our children
will help us out of these dark caves.

Taste Its Bleeding

Genesis 22

Take Sarah and Hagar.
Forget angels.
Wrestle instead with words.
Turn the text over and over.
Kick it in its shins, bruising it;
clutch exposed skin,
scraping it under your nails.
Bite its neck; taste its bleeding.
Only then will you understand
why Sarah drove poor Hagar out,
wretched sign of servitude to men,
of selfhood known only through motherhood.
Then you can reject all slavery
and not the slave, as Sarah did,
and understand mothering writ large.
Then you can exorcise your own,
the real demons.

Tamar

II Samuel 13

They always seduce us with their needs.
That which is assigned is twice taught.
Nurturing becomes second nature.
Wife, daughter, sister,
through the centuries of faithless fathers,
teaching hungry minds,
serving heaping bowls or rice
to a starving world,
withholding sons from wars.
A baby cries and we lactate,
as natural as making love.
When they learn this,
there will be no more forced entry,
no violations of these temples.
Gently touching our hems,
they will be healed.

Couvade For Jephthah's Daughter

Judges 11:29-40

So I told my sisters:
"Warn your daughters
about rushing into the arms
of fathers returning from war.
Even the flush of victory
cannot remove their taste for blood.
We are the expiation
for their foreign carnage.
If we give them sons or grandsons
to vindicate us in this ageless
totem ritual, we will forever
be victims of their misplaced vows
to a male diety. Apparently
the father who sacrifices a child
is answerable to no one."

And my sisters said to me:
"For four days each year
we will lament the virgin daughters
bound to death by duty.
Secretly, for four nights
as spring leaps to summer,
summer dances to fall,
autumn undresses to cold winter
who always dies to spring,
we will depart from men
and find our promise
in each other's arms.
For this they will burn us
as witches, call us
man-haters."

I ask you,
who is it hates who?

STATION NINE: JESUS FALLS A THIRD TIME

Despite the lack of biblical evidence for Jesus falling, tradition places three falls along the sorrowful route. Numerologists would point out the theological and symbolic importance of the number three. Perhaps most significant would be the Trinitarian formula for describing the Godhead.

This formula, formalized in the fourth century, is traditionally referred to as "Father, Son, and Holy Spirit (or Holy Ghost), although there has always been controversy surrounding it. That controversy is currently being renewed by the demands of feminist theologians that any description of the God head include a feminine principle (not because God is seen as a female human, but because they object to God being seen only as a male human and the balance of male and female might assist in the deanthropomorphizing of God). Some feminists are suggesting addition of a fourth person: Shekinah, or Sophia (Wisdom). Others insist that Mary be included along with "Father" and "Son" either by adding her as a fourth persona, or by gender-liberating the term "Father" and making it "Parent" to include both masculine and feminine principles.

Other controversies suggest a depersonalizing, degenderizing, dehumanizing of the "persons" so that emphasis is placed on their activity rather than on a human image of that activity: for example, Creator, Liberator, Sustainer instead of Father, Son, Holy Spirit, or Word, Weal, and Wisdom. Possibilities are unlimited, as is God.

The falls of Jesus on the Via Dolorosa serve to confirm unmistakably the fact of his full humanity, denial of which was an early gnostic heresy. It was that heresy — the denial of Jesus' full humanity and therefore of his dual nature as God and human — that led to the formulation of the more "theologically correct" Nicene Creed.

JESUS FALLS A THIRD TIME

From the Eighth Station on, the sites are on, or in,
buildings which did not exist
at the time of Jesus' journey to Golgotha...
This entire part of the city was outside the main walls.
Much later, every inch of the top of the hill was venerated
and marked by a chapel, convent, or monastery.
We must backtrack now to the main road
and climb very steep steps.
At the top, we are actually on the roof
of The Church of the Holy Sepulchre.

On this roof is a Coptic monastery,
maintained by monks for the last 300 years.
I was told that the monks, who come as young men,
spend their entire lives
in this compound and the church below;
and never leave once they have entered.

Here we see another pillar,
this one stooped, embedded in a wall, but standing.
Here, when the site was open hillside,
Jesus would have been about 25 feet away
from the point of his death.

Since the church now encloses the site,
we must pass through the tiny rooftop Coptic Chapel,
(large groups backtrack and go around it,) and enter
The Church of the Holy Sepulchre by the front door.

The floor of the church is but a few inches above
the actual rock hilltop below.
This yields an unusual internal architecture.
Immediately on entering, you go up about 20 steep stairs.
There you are on a mezzanine with a vaulted ceiling.
At Station IX you stand outdoors on top of this ceiling.

At Step 9 in AA we make direct amends to people we have wronged, except
when to do so would injure others.

When The Body Fails Us

There is this thickening of the ankles,
the liver spots on arthritic hands,
and of course
the shortness of breath.
I could still dance some days though
if there were any partners.
There's less hair where it should be
and more where it shouldn't,
like something is being reversed.
The dust sits longer now on bookshelves,
and funerals of friends are much too frequent.
Christmas card lists are shorter,
and so are shopping trips.
Food is no more fun,
and this driver's license expiration
may be the last.
Doctor's bills, oh Lord, and pills,
and living wills ...

what did you say, dear?

Code Blue

*For Ron Nofziger
and Archie Lawrence
Hillcrest Hospital Chaplains*

Surf the tide of life.
Heart deep, ride its waves.
Concentric rooms of sleep, aware,
sleep, aware: this one too young
to bear this aged woe, another
older than he never should nor
ever be to live this going on
I pray to stop which either start
so terminal we be
when we go home from here.

"Code Blue" is a hospital term for a patient in the last few minutes of being kept clinically alive by exhaustive technical applications. The excruciatingly exquisite nuance of the deathbed prayer is described here.

Station Ten: The Dividing Of The Garments

And when they had crucified him, they divided his clothes among themselves by casting lots; then they sat down there and kept watch over him.

Matthew 27:35-36

And they offered him wine mixed with myrrh; and he did not take it. And they crucified him, and divided his clothes among them, casting lots to decide what each should take.

Mark 15:23-24

And they cast lots to divide his clothing.

Luke 23:34b

When the soldiers had crucified Jesus, they took his clothes and divided them into four parts, one for each soldier. They also took his tunic; now the tunic was seamless, woven in one piece from the top. So they said to one another, "Let us not tear it, but cast lots for it to see who will get it." This was said to fulfill what the scripture says, "They divided my clothes among themselves, and for my clothing they cast lots.

John 19:23--25
See also Psalm 22:18

See also Exodus 28, which describes priestly garments and how they are to be made. "It shall have in it an opening for the head in the middle of it, with a woven binding around the opening, like the opening in a coat of mail, so that it may not be torn."

Exodus 28:32

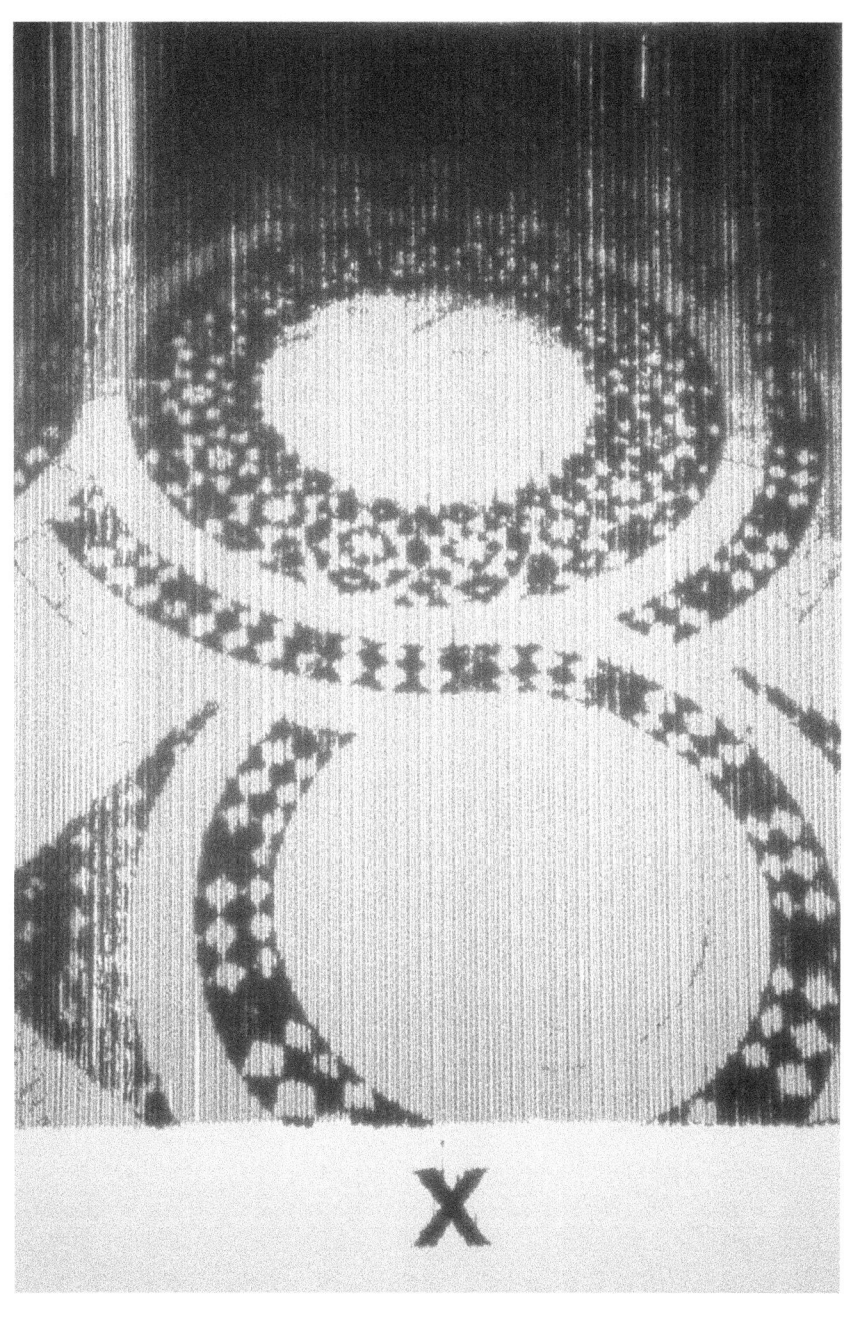

THE DIVIDING OF THE GARMENTS

Stations X, XI, XII, XIII
are all adjacent to one another
in an area about the size of a three car garage.

Station X is the place where the guards cast lots for Jesus' robe.

There is a mosaic in the ceiling depicting this,
but a painting of the mosaic floor seemed more appropriate.

Today the floor is inlaid with tile.

Just below this floor is the earth
on which the dice were cast.

AA's Step Ten is a continuation of our personal inventory, and, when we are wrong, acknowledging it.

The Seamless Robe

An ace in math, I mastered factors,
sine, cosine, diameter, perimeter,
triangles, trapezoids, cylinders and cubes,
square roots, shortest distances, logarithms,
arcs and angles, parallels and tangents,
calculated speed, volume and weight
as if each problem stood for something larger,
something more. Eternal verities
with unlimited applications.
My love for figures faltered once
when a simple division had no end,
but factored out behind that decimal
forever. It was infinity that did me in.
Infinity symbolized by the figure 8,
like the one in tile on the floor
above where the dice were cast. Like
the curved rim of the outer ear.
Like families, nations, races and the church;
some things were never meant to be divided.

Station Eleven: The Crucifixion

And when they came to a place called Golgotha (which means Place of a Skull), they offered him wine to drink, mixed with gall; but when he tasted it, he would not drink it. And when they had crucified him, they divided his clothes among themselves by casting lots; then they sat down there and kept watch over him.

Matthew 27:33-36

Then they brought Jesus to the place called Golgotha (which means the place of a skull). And they offered him wine mixed with myrrh; but he did not take it. And they crucified him, and divided his clothes among them, casting lots to decide what each should take. It was nine o'clock in the morning when they crucified him.

Mark 15:22-25

When they came to the place which is called The Skull, they crucified Jesus there with the criminals, one on his right and one on his left. Then Jesus said, "Father, forgive them, for they do not know what they are doing."

Luke 23:33 - 34a

So they took Jesus, and carrying the cross by himself, he went out to what is called The Place of the Skull, which in Hebrew is called Golgotha. There they crucified him, and with him two others, one on either side, with Jesus between them. Pilate also had an inscription written and put on the cross. It read, "Jesus of Nazareth, the King of the Jews." Many of the Jews read this inscription, because the place where Jesus was crucified was near the city; and it was written in Hebrew, in Latin, and in Greek. Then the chief priests of the Jews said to Pilate, "Do not write 'The King of the Jews,' but 'This man said, I am King of the Jews.'" Pilate answered, "What I have written, I have written." When the soldiers had crucified Jesus, they took his clothes and divided them into four parts, one for each soldier.

John 19:17 - 23a

The Crucifixion

The place of The Crucifixion
is marked by a silver altar,
a gift from the Grand Duke of Tuscany in 1609...

The silver altar covers the true altar,
the earth on which the blood was spilled.

It was on the earth that the nails were driven in,
while the cross was still on the ground,
before it was hoisted into place.

At Step 11 of the AA Program, we seek through prayer and meditation to improve our conscious contact with our higher power, seeking knowledge of God's will for us and the courage and power to do it.

The Reckoning

"Measure the color of days around your mother's death."

– Ellen Kort

Who would have thought that day
the visiting poet would prescribe
this autumn incantation,
this windy winding of the path to grief?

God calls. You have to answer.
Annunciation always stirs the universe;
tidal waves in veins and earthquakes
in our hearts.

One child curled up now sleeps with God;
another moves in dark auroras
toward that silence.
I have come to the Forest of Peace
to write this poem for Ike and Fran.

Brilliant leaves fall helter-skelter
at my feet.
I thought I'd be writing poems
on my own mother's dying; but no...
each day has its own reckoning.

For Ike and Fran Lazar; the day of Ike's death and Fran's ordination, 10-18-92

The Dog Who Dreamed Of Dying

The ridge of her spine jerks
against my hip. Her paws
tuck under, grabbing air
like earth beneath her dream.
Now she lunges at the throat
of the man with whiskey breath.
Her tongue is green
like sheep's tongues in New Mexico.
Her hair falls out in clumps.
Her bark becomes a yelp,
like the seals when the first club strikes.
She falls to the ground at his feet.
Roo! Roo! Roo!
Her lips peel back
as her flesh vacates her bones.
The man turns into a metal mantis.
His tongue is black; it dips
again and again
pumping black blood from the soil.
I startle awake.
My sheets are stained with blood.

Sophia Mandala

(For Mary Jane Lundy and all the other women persecuted for attending the "Re-Imagining" Conference)

> *"Can't we just get along?*
> —Rodney King

Those of us who line up too hard and fast
at one pole of the divine Circle
cannot know our own potential
rounded out in our compelled enemies. We
worship fragments, chopping off our own limbs
to fit our little image of Ultimate Beyond-Self,
not knowing we are never fully ourselves
til we reach into our far limits. Whatever
crosses borders is the breathing of time.
That breath, healing both ways, is God.

Godvoice wakes in virgin matrix,
limning fresh language from dark depths of self.
New begettings by women stirred by Spirit speech
brings new designs of mutuality, warm bodies
of thought and act, earth stretches of sky reaches.
We change the money-tables into altars
where no doves are garrotted, no lamb flesh burned
but gifts displayed of thought and dream
arrayed in tongue and touch and tear.

With the final cross emptied, the last necessary
blood spilled, birth waters breaking from the side
of Lamb baptize a new beginning, amniotic blessing
of ancient essence new substance, how these wineskins
swell with birthings. These new motherings
spread the wings of soul past rainbow archings
into new lovings, jubilee of wisdom's daughters.

Mandala is a Sanskrit word meaning "to have possession of one's essence." It is a sacred circle with a center point, a universal image that has long been a source of the experience of oneness and wisdom. It uses symbolic forms to draw out truth from the unconscious. These symbolic forms help connect our inner life to our outer life.

Station Twelve: Jesus Dies

From noon on, darkness came over the whole land until three in the afternoon. And about three o'clock Jesus cried with a loud voice, "E'li, E'li, le-ma sa-bach! tha-ni?" that is, "My God, my God, why have you forsaken me?" When some of the bystanders heard it, they said, "This man is calling for Elijah." At once one of them ran and got a sponge, filled it with sour wine, put it on a stick, and gave it to him to drink. But the others said, "Wait, let us see whether Elijah will come to save him." Then Jesus cried again with a loud voice and breathed his last.

Matthew 27:45-50

When it was noon, darkness came over the whole land until three in the afternoon. At three o'clock Jesus cried out with a loud voice, "E'lo-i, E'lo-i, le-ma sa-bach' tha-ni?" which means, "My God, my God, why have you forsaken me?" When some of the bystanders heard it, they said, "Listen, he is calling for Elijah." And someone ran, filled a sponge with sour wine, put it on a stick, and gave it to him to drink, saying, "Wait, let us see whether Elijah will come to take him down." Then Jesus gave a low cry and breathed his last. And the curtain of the temple was torn in two, from top to bottom. Now when the centurion, who stood facing him, saw that in this way he breathed his last, he said, "Truly this man was God's Son."

Mark 15: 33-39

One of the criminals who were hanged there kept deriding him and saying, "Are you not the Messiah? Save yourself and us!" But the other rebuked him, saying, "Do you not fear God, since you are under the same sentence of condemnation? And we indeed have been condemned justly, for we are getting what we deserve for our deeds, but this man had done nothing wrong." Then he said, "Jesus, remember me when you come into your kingdom." He replied, "Truly I tell you, today you will be with me in Paradise." It was now about noon, and darkness came over the whole land until three in the afternoon, while the sun's light failed; and the curtain of the temple was torn in two. Then Jesus, crying with a loud voice, said, "Father, into your hands I commend my spirit." Having said this, he breathed his last. When the centurion saw what had taken place, he praised God and said, "Certainly this man was innocent!"

Luke 23:39 - 47

After this, when Jesus knew that all was now finished, he said (in order to fulfill the scripture), "I am thirsty." A jar full of sour wine was standing there. So they put a sponge full of the wine on the branch of hyssop and held it to his mouth. When Jesus had received the wine, he said, "It is finished." Then he bowed his head and gave up his spirit.

John 19:28 - 30

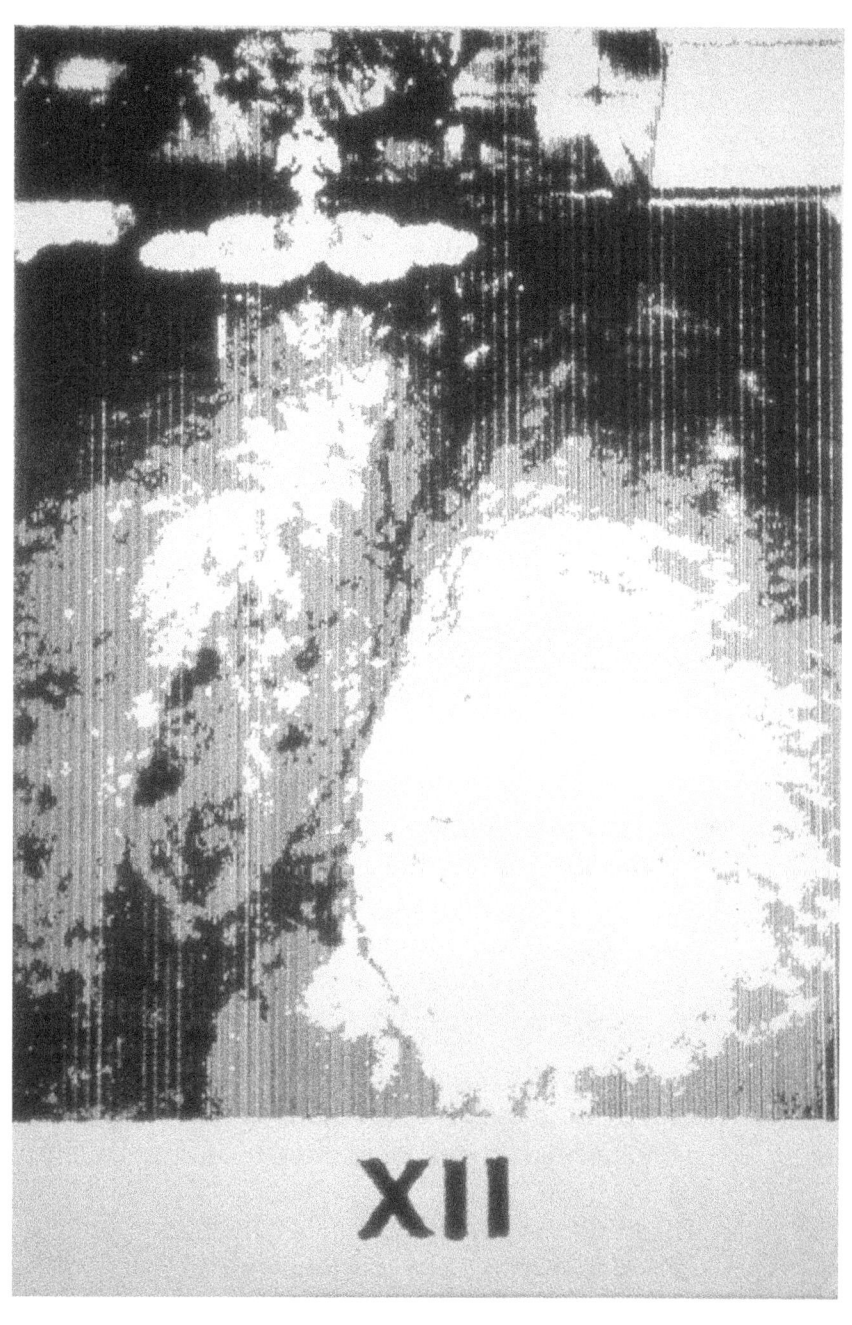

JESUS DIES

Station XII is marked by incredibly ornate mosaics,
altars, candelabra, paintings and sculptures.

All this directs one's attention to a very small altar,
really a tiny mantelpiece, about two feet off the floor.
In the floor under this altar is a gold ring,
about two feet in diameter.

In the center of this gold ring is a hole
about the size of a softball.

To reach it, you must be on your knees
(as well you probably are, in your mind and heart,
when you think about the events of 2,000 years ago at this site).

You kneel and peer through the hole. It is black.
You can see nothing, but you reach in
and down about six inches, and you touch the Rock of Calvary.

It is cool, slightly damp, smooth.
It dawns on you what you are doing.
You shudder with a sense of awe.

This is not an icon, an image or a picture,
a devotional or a ritual.
This is it.

Near the opening in the floor through which you reach
to touch the rock is a flat panel of glass,
about the size of a small coffee table, on which burns a lamp.

Through this panel you can see the rock
which you have just touched.
You pull your hand out a different person.

At Step Twelve of AA, having had a spiritual awakening or transformation as a result of the previous steps, we try to carry the message to others, and to practice these principles in all our affairs hereafter.

The Place of a Skull

> *"It all comes
> in whatever you got left."*
> —Meridel LeSueur

Meridel knew her dog was dying,
this half-wolf, half-domestic creature,
with its aged head resting in Mendel's lap
in that suburban Minneapolis back yard.
The moment the dog died
all the captive dogs in the neighborhood
gave out a piercing howl. Meridel calls it
the "simultaneity of ancestral memory."

We buried her on the riverbank
beneath a pile of fallen autumn leaves
because the frozen ground
was too hard to break.
In the spring Meridel returned
to find only its sun-bleached skull,
which now rests on her desk as a paperweight.
But dozens of bird nests in the tree branches
by the river sparkled in the sun
from the golden hair of the dog
woven in among the twigs.

Hunger Strikes

Hunger has settled in their hearts
forever. There is no end to it.
(The laughing plates desire
only to be clean, to clink
against each other in the sink.)

Whatever food is brought is eaten
right away, no waiting
for the host to eat, the guest
to take a seat, the blessing said.
No silent toasting of the dead.

Their sex goes first.
The body cannot reproduce
which does not eat. And so
it loosens its hold on the hair,
empty eye sockets fill with air,

and sight turns inward, toward the sea
of silence in the blood.
The navel is a sinkhole
sucking in the belly. These fasting feet
will never march a Belfast street.

The ribcage misses the lung's caress,
the hands begin to flutter
like severed wings of butterflies.
Where does water go when it dies?

Bathsheba's Confession

(In collaboration with Will Inman)

It is not that I deny biting the apple.
It is just that I don't like having to apologize
for loving anyone.

I was there when he arranged to have my husband killed.
When his son raped his daughter,
another son killed the rapist brother.
I heard him pray for the dying child,
mourn for the dead child, write poems, dance,
sing songs of praise to God.

So goes our lives toward center calm,
speaking till the unspeakable is spoken,
embracing all by embracing nothing.
We always return to the transient world naked,
on our knees, bleeding. Who suffers, passes;

who passes, suffers. We are human,
danced dazed down seasons and pulses,
human rooted in cries of other humans.
We can't help it, we cry. These are our weak
lovings. Show us the greater love.

There is no hell worse
than watching a loved one suffer.
So we confess, God,
we cannot bear to watch this dying.
God's death must be our hell.
We wonder if any of it does any good.

Yes, Doing is being; being is doing.
All begins with nothing; yes.
The heaviest stones can be moved.
It is done. Once and for all. Yes.

Station Thirteen: Jesus' Body Is Taken Down From The Cross

When it was evening, there came a rich man from Arimathea, named Joseph, who also was a disciple of Jesus. He went to Pilate and asked for the body of Jesus; then Pilate ordered it to be given to him. So Joseph took the body and wrapped it in a clean linen cloth and laid it in his own new tomb, which he had hewn in the rock. He then rolled a great stone to the door of the tomb and went away. Mary Magdalene and the other Mary were there, sitting opposite the tomb.

Matthew 27:57-62

When evening had come, and since it was the day of Preparation, that is, the day before the sabbath, Joseph of Arimathea, a respected member of the council, who was also himself waiting expectantly for the Kingdom of God, went boldly to Pilate and asked for the body of Jesus. Then Pilate wondered if he were already dead; and summoning the centurion, he asked him whether he had been dead for some time. When he learned from the centurion that he was dead, he granted the body to Joseph. Then Joseph brought a linen cloth, and taking down the body, wrapped it in the linen cloth, and laid it in a tomb that had been hewn out of the rock. He then rolled a stone against the door of the tomb. Mary Magdalene and Mary the mother of Jesus saw where the body was laid.

Mark 15:42-47

Now there was a good and righteous man named Joseph, who, though a member of the council, had not agreed to their plan and action. He came from the Jewish town of Arimathea, and he was awaiting expectantly for the Kingdom of God. This man went to Pilate and asked for the body of Jesus. Then he took it down, wrapped it in a linen cloth, and laid it in a rock hewn tomb where no one had ever been laid. It was the Day of Preparation, and the sabbath was beginning. The women who had come with him from Galilee followed, and saw the tomb, and how his body was laid. Then they returned, and prepared spices and ointments.

Luke 23:50-56a

After these things, Joseph of Arimathea, who was a disciple of Jesus, though a secret one because of his fear of the Jews, asked Pilate to let him take away the body of Jesus. Pilate gave him permission; so he came and removed his body. Nicodemus, who had at first come to Jesus at night, also came, bringing a mixture of myrrh and aloes, weighing about a hundred pounds. They took the body of Jesus and wrapped it with the spices in linen cloths, according to the burial custom of the Jews. Now there was a garden in the place where he was crucified, and in the garden there was a new tomb in which no one had ever been laid. And so, because it was the Jewish Day of Preparation, and the tomb was nearby, they laid Jesus there.

John 19:38-42

JESUS' BODY IS TAKEN DOWN FROM THE CROSS

Next to the opening in the floor
through which you reach to touch the Rock of Calvary,
is an altar with a glass case containing
a 16th-century statue of the Sorrowful Virgin,
presented by the Queen of Portugal in 1778.
This Station is actually located between
Station XI and Station XII.

Art about art.
Behind the doors lie chapels which are encrusted with art.

I didn't want simply to make "a painting
of other people's paintings."

Plus, coming from a Presbyterian/Disciple of Christ tradition,
pictures and icons have never been
a significant part of worship for me.

The real art here lies in the journey, which begins and ends in
bright lights (Stations I and XIV),
via the melancholic darkness of the doors,
pillars, walls, floor and symbols.

The broken rock of Calvary is covered by the art.
Uncover the art and you find the broken rock,
the broken body.

Doomsday

The pope doesn't want any test-tube babies.
No fielding of the womb by laser beams,
no splitting of the egg by sound waves,
no loving word to call this seed to life.
He refuses to enter the woman.
She decides to become what she needs.
The egg, round and fertile, like the earth,
fragrant and full, like the woman,
divides.
Two divided by two is one.
The child is a girl.
"It is not mine," he shouts!
The egg becomes an eight,
laying on its side,
twin-chromosomed double helix,
like the curved rim of the external ear.
She grows up and marries her shadow,
becomes father and mother,
lives happily ever after,
whole within herself.
The boy does not survive the test tube.
He must have a womb around him
since he does not have one inside him.
Didn't he know this "
when he made
the atom bomb?

Life After Death?

> *"It is the secret of the world that all*
> *Things subsist, and do not die,*
> *only retire a little from sight, and*
> *afterwards return again."*
> Ralph Waldo Emerson

I have to admit, I have my own theories about
how it all began and what gives it meaning,
what E=mc/2 means about relativity,
how actions produce equal and opposite
reactions; I understand gravity and electricity
and how ontogyny recapitulates phylogyny.
I know what's valuable and what's not,
why people do what they do, where things lead,
when to speak or listen; how to act in most situations,
who or what is responsible for most social pathologies,
what to do to address racism, sexism, crime, acid rain,
        family violence, war, despair, rape, deforestation,
        militarism, poverty, ageism, homophobia, poverty,
        abortion, ignorance, and rampant materialism,

but I still don't know what happens next.

Station Fourteen: Jesus' Body Is Laid In The Tomb

See the same Gospel texts as Station XIII.

Arise, shine;for your light has come, and the glory of the Lord has risen upon you. For darkness shall cover the earth, and thick darkness the peoples; but the Lord will arise upon you, and his glory will appear over you. Nations shall come to your light, and kings to the brightness of your dawn. Lift up your eyes and look around; they all gather together, they come to you; your sons shall come from far away, and your daughters shall be carried on their nurses' arms. Then you shall see and be radiant; your heart shall thrill and rejoice...

Isaiah 60:1-5b

Jesus said to her, "I am the resurrection and the life; Those who believe in me, even though they die, will live, and everyone who lives and believes in me will never die. Do you believe this?"

John 11:25 - 26

For additional texts on resurrection, see also: Psalm 49:15; Isaiah 26: 19; Ezekiel37; Matthew 22:23-32; Luke 20: 27-38; Mark 12: 24-27; Matthew 11:22-24 and 12:41-42; Acts 23: 6-8; I Corinthians 15:12-24; I Thessalonians 4:13-18; Phillippians 3: 20; the entire book of Revelations.

Now we go back down steep stairs to "street level"
and walk past the stone on which Christ's body was anointed...
It is a marble slab now surrounded by candles.
This is not an "official" Station of the Cross,
but is often venerated by pilgrims.

About 50 feet away is an ornate marble structure
a bit larger than a family mausoleum.
This is still within the larger building of
The Church of the Holy Sepulchre itself.

You can walk completely around this tomb/structure.

This location is under the province
of the Greek Orthodox Church
and is lavishly ornate and highly decorated.

There is an antechamber which holds 4-6 people.
One must stoop to enter the actual tomb.
Once inside, the ceiling is high enough
for you to to stand upright.
It provides room for 1 or 2 people.

There, about 30 inches off the ground, is a marble slab
on which the body of Jesus rested until that morning
we celebrate on Easter Sunday.

I tried to leave much to the imagination. This is as it should be.

Because whatever else is the case, though it is a tomb,
Jesus is not here.

JESUS' BODY IS LAID IN THE TOMB

LAMENTATIONS - A LITANY

*When the air cleared in Jonestown, British Guyana
there were over 900 bodies rotting in the sun.*

— Tulsa World

1: Woe the bloody sacrifice
2: Woe the rape of the mother earth!
3: Woe the soil, drenched with salty tears!
All: Hear our lamentation bleat
where the dense rain forests
carry drumbeats for miles
on the weight of the air near the earth.
1: We have sent this message before.
2: It is the dirge of the death of god,
whose bones lie bleached
on this ziggurat
erected in linear time
toward a deaf deity.
3: We shout our shame
for the patriarch Abraham
who sold our Sarah to the pharoah
for the price of his safety!
1: We cry for the rape of the Sabine women,
the wrenching of the babes
from the breast of Jerusalem!
2: We keen for the waters
running red, running black,
La Llarona searching endlessly
for her dead children.
All: Come back father,
Come back mother.
1: Woe the sword
that slices tongues for silence,
2: Woe the word
that calls no more
into the bowels of the earth
for her daughter.
3: La la la la la la la la!
(la la la la la la la la!)
1: Oooooooo my children,
2: Oooooooo my babes,
3: Oooooooo my swollen breasts
that rise into the clouds of nitrogen
left by the bombs!
1: Woe my womb

       that shrivels like a seed
       in sour soil, wasted water,
       gasping in the polluted air!
All: Oooooooo my children,
       Ooooooooo my babes,
       Ooooooooo my swollen breasts
  1:   La la la la la la la la!
All: (la la la la la la la la!)
  1:   At the end is the word,
       and the word said
  2:   Oooooooo my children,
  3:   Ooooooo my babes,
  1:   Ooooooo my swollen breasts
  2:   La la la la la la la la!
All: (la la la la la la la la!)
  3:   At the end is the word.
All: Ooooooooo

("La" is Swahili for "No"!)

The Dance Of The Zygotes

sotto voce
        in the wasted breath of the spoiled air
        in the caved-in mines of the sunken harbors,
        in the flooded earth of the sperm-bed soil,
        in the dark mined caverns of eroded hills,
        in the meiotic splitting of the earth's chromosomes,
        in the zygomorphic spheres of the earth's synapsis,

crescendo
        where the zygospores rest in mitotic dreams,
        where the gametes reach for the homologous gametes,
        where the zygotene move toward a zygomorphic union,
        where the gametes begin a chimerical chiasma,
        where the zygotes wiggle in a meiotic dance,
        where the chimeras leap in the bouyant air,

allegro
        then the language forms on the zygomorphic lips,
        then the sounds emerge from the singing zygotene,
        then the mitotic gametes do a zygomatic dance,
        then the cells crossing over form a chiasmatic ring,
        then the sperm and the ovum do their chromosomal whirl,
        then the zygotes form a circle in the bowl of the air,

piano forte
        and the women and the women and the men and the men,
        and the women and the men, and the men and the women,
        do the dance, do the dance,
        do the dance, do the dance,
        do the dance, do the dance,
        do the dance, do the dance

chi-as-ma — X-shaped configuration, crosspiece or cross-shaped configuration of paired chromatide visible in the diplotene or meiotic prophase and considered the cytological equivalent of genetic crossing-over.

chi-me-ra — A fire-breathing she-monster in Greek mythology having a lion's head, a goat's body, and a serpent's tail; an imaginary monster compounded of incongruous parts; an unrealizable dream; an individual, organ, or part consisting of tissues of diverse genetic constitution and occurring especially in plants and most frequently at a graft union.

gam-ete — A mature germ cell possessing a haploid chromosome set and capable of initiating formation of a new individual by fusion with another gamete.

ho-mol-o-gous — Having the same relative position, value, or structure; exhibiting biological homology; having the same or allelic genes with genetic loci usually arranged in the same order; belonging to or consisting of a chemical series whose members exhibit homology; derived from or developed in response to organisms of the same species.

ho-mol-o-gy - a similarity often attributable to common origin; likeness in structure between parts of different organisms due to evolutionary differentiation from the same or a corresponding part of a remote ancestor; the relation existing among the elements in the same group of the periodic table.

mei-o-sis — The representation of a thing as less than it actually is in order to compel greater esteem for it (understatement); the cellular process that results in the number of chromosomes in gamete-producing cells being reduced to one half and that involves a reduction division in which one of each pair of homologous chromosomes passes to each daughter cell and a miotic division occurs.

mi-to-sis —a process that takes place in the nucleus of a dividing cell, involves typically a series of steps consisting of prophase, metaphase, anaphase, and telephase, and results in the formation of two new nuclei each having the same number of chromosomes as the parent nucleus.

syn-ap-sis — The association of homologous chromosomes with chiasma formation that is characteristic of the first meiotic prophase and is held to be the mechanism for genetic crossing-over.

zy-go-ma — To join; the zygomatic arch is the arch of borne that extends along the front or side of the skull beneath the or bit.

zy-go-mor-phc — Bilaterally symmetrical and capable of division into essentially symmetrical halves by only one longitudinal plane passing through the axis.

zy-go-spore — A plant spore that is formed by union of two similar sexual cells; usually serves as a resting spore and produces the sporophytic phase of the plant.

zy-gote — A cell formed by the union of two gametes; the developing individual produced from such a cell.

zy-go-tene — The synaptic stage in meiosis in which homologous chromosomes pair intimately.

Stations

or

A 14-STEP PROGRAM TO CONQUER EXISTENTIALIST ANGST

With gratitude to George Santana and Jim Bransford
"A Word that breathes distinctly has not the power to die."
—Emily Dickinson

1. Though living
    I am powerless to live
    and though I may at any moment die
    I am powerless to die.
    Altogether, in every instant
    in every particular
    I am in the hands of some alien
    and inscrutable power.
    The action by which I am
    makes it truer to say
    that I am being lived
    than that I live.
    I live but do not have the power to live.
    Even my parents had not the power
    to elect me into being.
    Though they willed a child
    and consented to me
    they did not will me
    this I, thus and so.

2. And so also I now
    though I will to be no more as I
    but will instead the being of that
    power of being
    into my being
    cannot elect myself out of being
    if the inscrutable power
    by which I am
    elects otherwise

3. The radical act
    by which I came into being
    is unique with me
    though repeated by trillions of others.
    My particular coming into being
    has no history with me nor pattern

          nor analogies nor contexts within me
          to help me understand it.
          Because I can do nothing about it
          I am tempted to ignore it
          or avoid it or forget or deny it.

4. Though I encountered in my youth
          the inscrutable power
          by which I exist,
          I learned quickly
          not to attend to it,
          concentrate on it,
          or even talk about it.
          I learned to ask
          "What should I do?"
          instead of "what am I?"
          I ceased to exist as a self
          in the presence of my maker
          or of the action that made me.
          I began to exist as a self
          reflected in the eyes of others.
          I learned of a self
          in relation to other selves,
          to respond to all others,
          but not to that otherness
          by which the self is self.
          My body and mind,
          contracts and commitments,
          consciousness and communion
          were always with a third person.

5. When I fell out of grace
          with the third person
          I felt unfavored by the first person
          by the radical act
          that willed me into being.
          Losing myself in my self,
          the second person, in fields of forces,
          or systems of ideas,
          is no adequate response
          to the power by which
          my self exists.
          To do so does not take seriously (enough)
          the radical character
          of the action by which
          the self comes into being

       nor understand
       how its response to that action
       qualifies all its other responses.

6. If I call the power
       by which I am
                              (love)

       and if my devotion to such a power
       which affirms all being
       since it calls all being into being
       is called
                              (faith)

       then (faith) is my response
       to that radical act (love)
       that calls my self into being
       and determines thereby
       my response to other beings.

7. If I reject identification
       with any of the other powers
       such as (money)
       and all that such powers call into being
       I show no trust in such power
       nor in other beings
       who have trust in such power.
       Thus I cannot commit myself
       to (money), or to profit motive,
       to goods and possessions
       to slavery and violence,
       to fear, apathy, and despair
       and all things controlled by those powers.
       If those powers and authorities,
       their relationships and properties,
       keep me from being a self
       in relation to other selves
       in relation to the source of being
       and keeps the community of (faith)
       torn from the radical action that
       brought it into being (love)
       then I give my self
       in response to those powers (money)
       and not to that radical action (love)
       that calls all selves
       into being.

8. If I rely on (money)
    or on those selves who rely on (money)
    as the power
    that calls me into being
    then I
                              (sin)
    and my (sin) disrupts
    my being in communion
    with other beings
    in communion with
    that radical action
    that calls community into being
    and wrests my being
    from its source of being

9. As I respond in (faith)
    to that inscrutable power (love)
    that calls my self
    and all other selves
    into being
    I also respond
    within a community of (faith)
    (in varying degrees of trust and mistrust)
    to the being or act of being
    that wills all beings to respond
    by being
    selves
    in community.

10. My self
    is one self among all the selves
    with whom I share my being.
    It is a counterpart
    of the unity that lies beyond
    yet is expressed within
    all the other selves
    that act upon it.
    My self and its maker
    belong together.
    I am one within
    myself
    as I encounter
    the One
    in all that I encounter.

11. By that action
    whereby I am I
    in all the roles I play
    in response to all the systems and persons
    of action I encounter,
    I seek to be with the One
    within and beyond all the many
    and my response to every action
    is a response also to the One
    that is active in it.
    My response to the radical action (love)
    in all responses to finite actions
    means to seek one integrity of self
    among all the other integrities,
    means to be one responding self
    among all the selves,
    responding
    in universal community,
    whose center is neither in me
    nor any finite cause
    but is the transcendent
    and imminent ONE power and being
    that brings all being
    into being.

12. I find unity and community,
    identity and dignity,
    in my responsiveness
    to the action by which
    I came into being (love)
    and am my self,
    one I among many Ts,
    and in response to that action
    in all the actions which I encounter.
    To respond to that action
    is to respond to my maker,
    is to be responsible to other selves
    and other actions,
    is to be fully and finally
    my self coining into being.
    The self which is ONE in its self
    responds to all actions
    as expressive of the ONE action (love)
    that brought it into being.

13. And when I die
       as I know surely I will die
       as all selves die, as all Is die,
       then that (faith)
       which has been my radical response
       to that radical act (love)
       that calls all selves into being
       carries my being into a
       new kind of being
       along with all other selves
       who share that (faith)
       which being can neither be known
       nor understood until this being
       is lost into it
       and no longer lives in this being
       but surrenders to the new being.

14. This new being
       had already begun to transform
       the old being when
       the old being no longer willed
       to be the I but
       willed instead the being
       of that power of being (love)
       into its being. And then
       its new being will know
       the will of that inscrutable power
       and will be in being
       with that being
       forever
       in (faith) and
       in (love).
       All things were before I was
       and all things will be after I have been.
       It is not my being that made it so
       but it is my being that will continue to be
       by that power of all being in my being
       and it is this new being in my being
       that declares it to be so,
       even though (love)
       at its profoundest moments
       is silent.

Honest To God ... There Are Days

> *That truth is in order to goodness,*
> *and the great touchstone of truth,*
> *its tendency to promote holiness .*
> Presbyterian Book of Order

It's true that everyone lies.
Especially when they need a celestial linger
on their slippery knot. Lord, so big and shiny,
please please regard me just a little.
Remember how good I was last month, before
that bit of slippage with that feral cat
lurking around my birdfeeders.
The birds that begin before dawn crying domain,
eking out a song over the din of street traffikers
roaring their thoughtless speed amid my silence,
radios blaring something they think is music.
That man raking my leaves with his high ass
and long legs, brown skin, eyes and hair
that I pay with money for his labor
but want to give much more.
Forget that, and my lack of repentance.
Lord, make of me an apostle, a good one,
except maybe not one that does much anymore.
I can't be the one who says with any purpose,
"look, he's walking on water" since I can barely walk
on land. I might be able to say "he raises me daily
from my bed," though that is probably my main
half-hearted truth.
O evening, you tie ropes to my wrists each day.
I drink God's silence from my own deep wells.
And if my mouth opens, it's just woe, woe, woe
in self-pity and anger at a self-serving world.
Very the pain, or verify— either way,
drowning seems drawing, death made dearth,
and what I love most I've lost, given away,
or has been taken from me. The words eke out
and etch into the window panes, lucid in the breath,
but gone again once warmth recedes. I hang on
to facsimile, slim volumes that stack up like a ladder
to poetry--wait, I meant poverty. No, poetry.
 I admit, I'd rather go to the underworld
where the poet's tongue is cut out to account for her silence,
rather than undergo this world much further.
No, nothing so dramatic — I mean all this is gesture —

the cardinals can explain. Because when I untie
my heel's strap and reveal myself in the glory
of my shabby bedroom--such a cacophony of
oboe/oriole tones, reborn and showering all who call love
to the unlistening air with kisses
of the most exquisite insincerity, the crows will caw,
mockingbirds offer their crackling songs in all
the morning's noise, spinning out a song
I'm forgetting how to harmonize.
No, what you have, I have,
whatever it is that shouldn't be missed, but is, but was.
And one lesson I've learned: to calm the waves
and praise the company that my own shadow
casts on this last, difficult, unwilling Jonah journey.

Afterword

Probably the definitive, and certainly one of the most deeply spiritual descriptions of the *Stations of the Cross* and its meaning and impact is Caryll Houselander's *The Way of the Cross* (New York: Sheed and Ward, 1955). In that textbook of Christ's passion, Houselander is sure that "there are certain inevitable experiences which are common to us all... and from which none can escape. One of these is death. Another is love... and the price of love ... is suffering." (p. 6)

One of the earliest and most popular ways that attention was drawn to the suffering and death (called "passion") of Jesus Christ has been to retrace his journey to Calvary. "No doubt, the Christians of the original community must from time to time, with devout remembrance, have gone over again the road which Jesus then had to go. Before their inner eye there would come to life again that which had happened." (Romano Guardini, *The Way of the Cross*, New York: Benzinger Bros., 1932, p. 3)

Guardino describes the "doing of the stations", as it has come to be called, as follows: "he made his *statio*, which is to say, in primitive Church language, that he made a halt there with devout remembrance and with worshipful intent, and carried himself back to those times, (p. 4)

This pilgrimage became even more popular at the time of the Crusades (1095-1270), whenever more devout pilgrims began to visit the Holy Land from distant parts to retrace the steps of Jesus. It was seen as "one of the truest and purest of popular devotions: uniting picture and thought, outward action and inward disposition, historical truth and creative action of the believing imagination." (Guardini, p. 5) In fact, "Pope Alexander the Sixth assigned the Iubile and Stations to be had in sundrie provinces and countries." (Beacon, *Reliques of Rome*, 1563, quoted in *The Oxford English Dictionary*. Vol. X, Clarendon, 1933, p. 185.)

After the Moslems recaptured the Holy Land, such pilgrimages were too dangerous, but "a substitute pilgrimage, the Stations of the Cross, became popular outdoors throughout Europe. They represented critical events from Scripture or tradition of Jesus' journey to Calvary." (Greg Dues, *Catholic Customs and Traditions: A Popular Guide*, Mystic, CT: Twenty-Third Publications, 1973, p. 92.)

By the mid-eighteenth century, the stations were brought inside the churches, and became fixed at fourteen. Away was devised "of making pictures of the incidents of the way of sorrows, and of putting these in churches ... The Franciscans, in particular, were most active in this." (Guardini, pp. 4-5) The stations are a familiar part of many Roman Catholic structures to this day. In the 1960s, it became popular to add a fifteenth station representing the resurrection, since, as Houselander states, "the way of the cross though it leads to the tomb and dark sleep of death, leads on beyond it to the waking morning of resurrection and the everlasting springtime of life." (p. 7) However, in most places the number of stations remains fourteen.

Since Lent, and also at times Advent, are considered seasons of penance, it was at these "high holy seasons" that the stations were most commonly traversed. Most frequently the walks through the stations took place biweekly, on Wednesday and Friday, although some of the most devout would travel them more frequently. Early Christian mystic, St.Bridget, was a case in point: "When she was at Rome... she wente every daye the Stacyons ordeyned by the churche." (Gascoign, *Life of St. Bridget in Myrr. our Ladye*,1873, p. iii.) A later Christian mystic, Countess Richmond, did three stations daily: "After dyner full truely she wolde goe her Statyons, to thre Aulters dayly." (Fisher, *Funeral Serm. C'tess Richmond*, Wks. 1876, p. 295)

Doing the stations was similar to confession, and secured for its traveler a certain blessing: "A general remission and pardon to assoille all that hadde made any a vowe to goo the Stacions of Jerusalem or to Rome." (Bale's *Chron., 1461*, in Town Chron., 1911,141.) Guardini says that doing the stations was "the most ancient of all popular devotions." (p. 3) Houselander brings the stations closer to home when she insists that "The Stations of the Cross are not given to us only to remind us of the historical Passion of Christ, but to show us what is happening now, and happening to each one of us." (p.4)

This theme is reiterated in Marion Crawford's description of Queen Beatrix and her Knight Gilbert, who "learned and understood that the cause of God lies not buried among the stones in any city, not even in the most holy city of all; forthe place of Christ's sufferings is in men's sinful hearts ..." (*Via Grucisi A. Romance of the Second Crusade*, New York: Grosset and Dunlap, 1898, p. 396.)

It is the suggestion of this book that the stations are a paradigm of stages of spiritual development or faith development. Because the Via Dolorosa represents the footsteps of Jesus Christ, it also represents what we all have in common with him - our humanity. As such, it becomes a minicosm for our own spiritual journey through life, its steps or stages representing those we experience in our spiritual growth and maturation. It is not exclusively Roman Catholic, although the "doing" of the stations came into existence at a time in history when virtually all Christendom was represented by the Roman Catholic Church.

We Protestants often forget that three-fourths of our own history is Roman Catholic (from the first to the fifteenth centuries), and only after the Great Reformation were there Roman Catholic and Protestant designations. We would do well to study early church, Patristic, and pre-Reformation history of the church in order to understand better our own roots of faith.

Often one does not recognize that one has been on a spiritual journey until the gift of maturity and retrospective occurs. It may be at Station Five or Station Ten; it may be at one's first fall, or one's encounter with one's parents (becoming a parent oneself), or at one's own death (or the death of a loved one, or near death experience) that the life journey is seen and understood as a spiritual one. It may never be recognized as such, but that doesn't change the fact that it has been happening, unless, of course, there is "arrested spiritual development" just as there is often arrested physical, social, or intellectual development.

In some cases, the journey is a constant wrestling with angels on the darkest nights, usually emerging wounded, but transformed, with a new name, a convolution (metanoia), convergence (conversion), or evolution. Fists are shaken at God, and bricks thrown at the church. But, as Thomas Merton so aptly said, "suddenly there is a point where religion becomes laughable. Then you decide that you are nevertheless religious."

If you look up "station" in *The Oxford English Dictionary*, you will find many thought-provoking descriptions:

(1) The action or posture of standing on the feet; manner of standing. ("Nature allows us two feet for the firmer station." Bulwer, *Anthropoment*, xxi, 234.)

(2) The condition or fact of standing still; assumption of or continuance in a stationary condition; opposed to motion. "Her motion and her station are as one. She shewes a body rather than a life." (Shakespeare, *Anthony and Cleopatra*, 1606, III, iii.) "The vacuity of both Heauiness and Lightnesse ... is rather the principle of station, than of Motion." (Fotherby, Atheom, II, xi, 1619) "Her life is a progress, and not a station." (Emerson, Ess., *Compensation*, 1841,122.)

(3) A halt; a stand. Now rare or obsolete."But now, my Soule, here let us make a Station, to view perspicuously this sad aspect." (Davies, *Holy Rhoade*, F36,1609.)

(4) "A portable Temple . . . which might be carried and removed, according to the stations and removes of Israel." (Heylin, *Eccl. Vind.*, II, ii, 117, 1657.)

(5) An act of a pageant or a mystery play."Fynallyof this stacon thus we mak a conclusyon." (1485, *Dighy Myst.*, 1882,II, 155.)

(6) The apparent standing still of a planet in its apogee or perigee. "The planets in their stations list'ning stood." (Milton, *Paradise Lost*, 1667, VII, 563)

(7) The stationary point, crisis, height.

(8) Standing-place, position; the place in which a thing stands or is appointed to stand; a point at which one stands to obtain a view; a position occupied (in other posture than standing); the kind of place in which an animal or plant is fitted to live; a naval station, harbor, or port, or the period of time for which a vessel is appointed for a specified time; a place where soldiers are garrisoned; a military post; the locality to which an official is appointed (a scientist, officer, preacher, etc); a metaphorical standing-place or position in a scale of estimation or dignity; a person's position in the world (employment,

economic class, etc.) position in the social scale (higher or lower).

(9) A stopping-place on a journey; a place of temporary abode during migration; a regular rest stop along a road.

(10) Ecclesiastical uses: a place at which clergy assemble; each of a number of holy places visited by pilgrims in fixed succession; a visit to a holy place, or an assembly held there for the purposes of devotion on the appointed day. Taking the way of Jesus to God. Choosing compassion: the love that suffers. Attempting to lift/eliminate the burdens and sorrows of the world. Falling, again and again. Knowing you can't go it alone. Standing in solidarity with your fellow suffering humans. Taking the way of Jesus to God.

BIBLIOGRAPHY

Brueggemann, Walter. *Finally Comes The Poet: Daring Speech for Proclamation*. Minneapolis, MN: Fortress Press, 1989.

Capps, Donald. *The Poet's Gift: Toward the Renewal of Pastoral Care*. Louisville: Westminster / John Knox Press, 1993.

Crawford, Marion. *Via Crucis: A Romance of the Second Crusade*. New York: Grosset and Dunlap, 1898.

Dues, Greg. *Catholic Customs and Traditions: A Popular Guide*. Mystic, CT: Twenty-Third Publications, 1973.

Gaffney, Patrick. *Mary's Spiritual Maternity*. Bay Shore, NY: Monfort Publications, 1976.

Gray, Elizabeth Dodson. *Sunday School Manifesto: In The Image Of Her?* Wellesley, MS: Roundtable Press, 1994.

Guardini, Romano. *The Way of the Cross*. New York: Benziger Bros., 1932.

Houselander, Caryll. *The Way of the Cross*. New York.Sheed and Ward, 1955.

Johnson, Elizabeth A. *She Who Is: The Mystery of God in Feminist Theological Discourse*. New York: Crossroad, 1993.

McAnally, Mary. *Family Violence: Poems on the Pathology*. La Jolla, CA: Moonlight Publications, 1982. (with accompanying dialogue enabler)

McFague, Sallie. *Metaphorical Theology: Models of God in Religious Language*. Philadelphia: Fortress Press, 1982.

New Revised Standard Version of the English Bible.Thomas Nelson, Inc. Nashville: Cokesbury, 1990.

The Oxford English Dictionary. Vol.X. Clarendon, 1933.

Parra, Nicanor. *Poems and Antipoems*. Edited by William Miller, New York: New Directions, 1958.

Swidler, Leonard. *Jesus Was A Feminist*" Catholic World. 1971.

The Twelve Steps -- ASpiritual Journey: AWorking Guide for Adult Children From Addictive and Other Dysfunctional Families —Based on Biblical Teachings. San Diego, CA: Recovery Publications, 1988.

Wahlberg, Rachel Conrad. *Jesus According To A Woman*. New York: Paulist Press, 1975.

Walker, Alice. *The Color Purple*. New York: Harcourt Brace Jovanovich Publishers, 1982.

Dear Reader:

Thank you for purchasing "STATIONS".

We hope you find it:

- Illuminating
- Instructive
- Inspiring

We also hope the poems and images within give you the EXPERIENCE of two profound journeys:

1. Stops along a difficult mile in Jerusalem, and
2. Steps on a longer road known as "life".

If you enjoyed this work and your online bookseller asks you for an opinion or a rating, please take a moment to guide others with your experience of this book. It means a lot and we appreciate it.

Sincerely,

Norman   Mary

Norman Dolph & Rev. Mary McAnally

GoodReadBooks, Inc.
service@GoodReadBooks.com

www.ingramcontent.com/pod-product-compliance
Lightning Source LLC
Chambersburg PA
CBHW061451040426
42450CB00007B/1318